OTHER REALITIES?

OTHER REALITIES?

The enigma of Franek Kluski's mediumship

by

ZOFIA WEAVER

www.whitecrowbooks.com

For Michael

Published and printed in the United States of America and the United Kingdom
by White Crow Books; an imprint of White Crow Productions Ltd.

For information, contact White Crow Books
at 3 Hova Villas, Hove, BN3 3DH United Kingdom,
or e-mail to info@whitecrowbooks.com.

Cover Designed by Butterflyeffect
Interior design by Velin@Perseus-Design.com

Paperback ISBN 978-1-910121-39-9
eBook   ISBN 978-1-910121-40-5

Non Fiction / Body, Mind & Spirit / Parapsychology

www.whitecrowbooks.com

CONTENTS

FOREWORD

One of the predictable though less serious consequences of the First World War was a surge in the Spiritualist movement in Britain and other parts of Europe and the English-speaking world. Many thousands of bereaved persons whose loved ones had been so senselessly slaughtered were desperate to receive from the beyond some hint that bereavement is not for ever and that some contact between the living and the dead may be possible even before the former 'pass over' to join the latter. And the 'spirit mediums' who catered for this yearning were not, as many would suppose, in all cases obvious charlatans. Some were interesting enough to attract the attention of leading members of societies devoted to the cautious and scientific investigation of these and other related phenomena, for example in Britain the Society for Psychical Research, in France the Institut Metapsychique and in Poland the Polish Society for Psychical Research.

It is customary to divide mediums into two broad categories, 'mental mediums,' who retail communications from the departed through automatic speaking or writing, or by means of 'clairvoyant' or 'clairaudient' perception of the spirits themselves, and 'physical mediums,' round whom centre peculiar physical happenings of various kinds, from raps to 'materializations,' which 'the spirits' can allegedly influence and direct so as to communicate with persons present at a séance. A very limited number of mediums have to some degree straddled both these categories.

One such was the Pole known as 'Franek Kluski' (1873-1943), a banker, and a successful author, playwright and poet. From early childhood he had been surrounded by odd happenings to which he seemingly became more or less accustomed, but he did not emerge as a medium until 1918 when he attended a sitting with a noted medium at a friend's house, and it became apparent that the happenings tended to centre round him rather than round the official medium. After this he began to hold sittings himself, never for any remuneration (of which he had no need) but for his own interest and that of friends and others in his orbit. Perhaps also he felt it a duty to help the bereaved, and to open his powers to scientific investigation. He did not seek publicity, and preferred to use a pseudonym. He was notably amenable to controls suggested by investigators (including sitting in complete nudity at a séance held for the French researchers Dr Gustave Geley and Professor Charles Richet).

If the numerous accounts of Kluski's sittings are to be believed, which I rather fear that in considerable part they are, he must, in terms of the matchless variety and astonishing nature of the phenomena he produced, have been the most remarkable medium of his time, probably of any time. And yet only a somewhat limited amount about him has filtered through to Western Europe and beyond. The main reason for this is quite simple. The bulk of the relevant literature is in Polish and has never been translated. Dr. Zofia Weaver is a native speaker of Polish, has long had an interest in psychical research (with particular reference to mediumship), is on the Council of the Society for Psychical Research, and has served as Editor of that Society's *Journal* and *Proceedings*. She is thus particularly well qualified to remedy this deficiency. Her book, though relatively brief, is admirably clear. It covers Kluski's life; its Polish background; the strange (sometimes almost crazily strange) phenomena that occurred not just at his sittings but sometimes during his ordinary day to day life; and some possible parallel cases. Above all it contains well-chosen sample translations from the copious original records of his sittings.

I would not dream of anticipating Dr. Weaver's materials and views. But I thoroughly recommend this fascinating and indeed ground-breaking book about a uniquely puzzling individual.

Alan Gauld

FROM THE AUTHOR

I have been familiar with the material about Kluski for well over twenty years. I did next to nothing about it and a paper and lecture for the Society for Psychical Research barely scratched the surface. The reason was simple: putting a great deal of time and effort into translating and researching the enormous store of material, which looked totally unbelievable, seemed like a waste of time.

Since my first encounter with Kluski, I have learnt a great deal more about other physical mediums, but also about similar phenomena being witnessed in other, non-mediumistic contexts. Above all, I have also become aware of a number of impressive experiments conducted by a variety of early researchers, often sane academics who, if we reject the hypothesis that they reported the truth about what they observed, had to be subject to some form of madness which inexplicably descends on independent groups of scientists, sometimes in their laboratories, leading them to make exactly the same malobservations. The alternative explanation is a conspiracy of lies which extends over different times and locations.

The mediumship of Franek Kluski is, to my knowledge, unique in its scale and range. He himself was in many ways, not least physically, different from most people. His mediumistic powers developed within a circle of people with particular gifts and at a special time, in circumstances which were unique in the history of physical mediumship. However, it is not the case that nothing like the phenomena reported here happens today: the scale and range may be unique, but the phenomena are not.

The main body of the material which follows is based on reports written or collated by Kluski's friend and regular séance participant, Norbert Okołowicz, published in Polish in 1926. His book is by now rare and the evidence it presents, unless made public, might well disappear without trace, or be subject to incomplete or distorted reporting and interpretation which is to be found in a number of sources relying on second-hand information. Putting the record straight is only fair to Kluski himself, particularly as he never sought any publicity, and to the men and women who did their best to report what they experienced as faithfully as they could, believing they were serving science. The material they produced is too extensive and too repetitive to publish in full, but I have tried to include a comprehensive and representative sample of Kluski's mediumship as it developed over a brief period of seven years (1918-1925).

Much of the material is as it was when I first read it - unbelievable. Or, unbelievable within reality as we know it. Much psychical research relies on minute effects and their statistical interpretation, sometimes making tiny punctures in the prevailing worldview. The evidence of Kluski (and quite a few others) tears that worldview apart. We may find the reports incredible but, perhaps, if we start asking what the world would have to be like for them to be true, we might at least learn where to look for clues to what might lie beyond.

ACKNOWLEDGMENTS

This book would not have been written without the friendly encouragement, support and advice of Alan Gauld, Julie and David Rousseau, its publisher, Jon Beecher, and above all my husband Michael. To all of you, my heartfelt thanks.

I never said it was possible. I only said it was true.

CHARLES RICHET

INTRODUCTION

PHYSICAL MEDIUMSHIP: THE REFUGE OF CHEATS AND SCOUNDRELS?

From the seventeenth century onwards, magic lantern shows and phantasmagorias produced impressive ghostly shows. From crude animations to sophisticated full-scale illusions, multiple, moving, hovering, transparent phantoms, shrouded in mists and vapours and aided by appropriate sound effects and settings, frightened and delighted their audiences. Throughout the nineteenth century magicians thought up increasingly complex shows and tricks, and one need only look at the number of TV programmes devoted to such wonders in the present to realise that we are as eager as ever to be awed and amazed in this way.

Magicians create powerful "magic" through optical and other illusions. They can make things appear and disappear, they can destroy and restore them, and they can make things float, change one into another, or penetrate one another. To produce magic, they need to be able to divert attention and to control the space in which the tricks are performed. They need to be good at the psychology of deception but, for large-scale illusions, they also need equipment; (mechanisms, wires, levers, magic lanterns, mirrors, lighting, cabinets, props, automatons, assistants)[1].

What can be done on stage cannot be done in an ordinary room, or even a local community hall. However, much can be achieved in darkness or semi-darkness particularly when the audience is willing to believe. The nineteenth century saw a great deal of such home-made productions, involving a tremendous amount of fakery by a variety of mediums.

There were complex reasons why mediumship, particularly physical mediumship with its raps, levitations, apports, phantoms and objects moving by themselves, the craze for table-turning, and the rise of the new religion of Spiritualism, produced enormous controversy in the nineteenth century, and its echoes continue to this day[2]. With magic tricks, we know where we are. We have given our consent to be deceived and the deceivers can be proud of their skill. With physical mediumship, in most investigated cases, (both in the early days and more recently) the deceived and the deceivers played a much more complex game of deception and self-deception based on a variety of motivations thereby cloaking whatever genuinely anomalous phenomena there might be in a haze of claims and counter-claims. Some of the strength of the opposition to mediums was, and is, based on genuine moral outrage at vulnerable people being duped, but the phenomena have always presented a challenge to much more than that: to the findings of science, to established religion and, above all, to ordinary common sense.

This is a book about Franek Kluski, a man whose unwilling and short-lived brush with mediumship during the 1920s has left perhaps the most spectacular and the most puzzling evidence on record. The most natural and rational reaction to such tales of wonder would be to dismiss them. If one is to be at least prepared to give them serious consideration, it needs to be shown that the obvious explanations of how these phenomena could be produced by conventional means are inadequate. Hence this brief excursion into the subject of how fake physical mediums produced their tricks in the early days of raising spirits.

---

[1] A very readable source of information on the subject is Jim Steinmeyer's *Hiding the Elephant.*

[2] Such as that caused by the Scole report, describing physical phenomena produced at a home circle in the 1990s in England (Keen et al, 1999).

Deception relies on the fact that people will infer a lot more than they actually see, especially under the right conditions and with the right expectations. The phenomena might involve crude manipulation of objects (at traditional séances those were often tambourines, bells or trumpets) with rods and limbs. Tables might levitate in response to nimble toes and cut-outs of hands could be made to look as if they were moving their fingers, while lights could be produced by using a variety of substances, such as phosphorus or ferrocerium. A willing audience might recognise spirits of the departed in wire masks covered with handkerchiefs, or painted faces draped with cheesecloth or netting. "Spirits" could rise and then disappear as the "ectoplasm", or white material, was rolled back and hidden. More elaborate and professional arrangements might involve areas with concealed entrances into the séance room or cabinet, substitution of pre-prepared paranormal objects, and any number of accomplices skilled in using luminous paint and producing the required effects.

In the words of Malcolm Gaskill, "Traditionally, materialization mediums had relied on props. [...] But props were difficult to use wherever pre-séance cabinet searches were conducted [...] and by 1930 fraudulent mediums on tour could safely use only what they could hide on their own bodies. Usually, this meant white cloth, but discreetly inflated balloons and rubber gloves also made an appearance. [...] The SPR Research Officer, the aristocratic C.V.C. Herbert, experimented by dragging a handkerchief attached to a length of cotton, slowly winding it towards him round the stub of a pencil. In a weak light, observers found the trick almost impossible to detect". (Gaskill 2001: 232)

Stricter controls would not necessarily prevent fraud. Sittings with a medium controlled by having her hands and legs held by participants might offer opportunities for creating a distraction (such as the need to sneeze) and making the controllers believe each of them is holding a different hand when they are both hanging on to the same one. One hand, elbow, or mouth, could be very effective, as Polish psychical researchers found when investigating a medium claiming to produce ectoplasm. The medium underwent a personal search with an examination of the orifices, and wore a swimsuit provided by the Polish Society for Psychical Research[3]. Controls involved holding hands by controllers,

---

[3] The Polish "Society for Psychical Research" [Towarzystwo Badań Psychicznych] was the name of the first of three similar societies established in Warsaw during the interwar period, and which finally all amalgamated

a red light, and taking photographs. Yet the ectoplasm turned out to be muslin on a black thread pulled by the teeth, and hand substitution had taken place. Fraud was revealed when a photograph was taken without the prior warning click which was demanded by the medium[4].

Experienced investigators were certainly always on the lookout for fakes. Julian Ochorowicz, psychologist, naturalist, inventor and psychical researcher (as well as an amateur magician), recounts the story of Charles Richet (a Nobel-prize winning physiologist) weighing a Mrs Williams, the "flower medium", before and after the show, with the difference in weight equalling the weight of the flowers distributed by the medium during the séance. Ochorowicz's experience with numerous mediums makes him very much aware of people's desire to believe. Where he sees a sheet and a glove, others recognise a human phantom, and blame Ochorowicz for producing bad vibrations. (Ochorowicz 1913-1915).

Hereward Carrington, an indefatigable investigator and author of a classic exposé of mediumistic tricks, *Physical Phenomena of Spiritualism*, tells us that "having sat many score, if not hundreds of times, with mediums I [...] had never seen one single manifestation of the physical order which I could consider genuine. On the contrary, I had always detected fraud, and, being an amateur conjurer myself, was enabled in nearly every instance to detect the modus operandi of the trick, usually the first time I saw it". (Carrington 1909: 154). Incidentally, his first sitting with Eusapia Palladino, a famous and controversial Italian medium, made him change his mind, more of which later.

Thus, there are plenty of grounds for believing that the somewhat unsavoury reputation which came to surround physical mediumship was justified. This view was strengthened by the stance taken by the

---

into one organisation in 1938. Since their members tended to belong to more than one society, and to participate in overlapping research activities, the organisational structures are often difficult to establish and seem less relevant to the modern reader. I therefore use the terms "Polish Society for Psychical Research", or "Polish SPR" to refer to the group of individuals involved in psychical research on a regular basis during the period in question.

[4] Reported in the journal of the Polish Society for Psychical Research, *Zagadnienia Metapsychiczne* [Metapsychical Issues] July/August/September 1924, No.3, pp. 161-172, and representative of the investigative skills of the researchers who sat with Kluski. The production of lights and levitations was eliminated at an earlier stage of the investigation as the controls became stricter.

founders of the Society for Psychical Research[5] after a series of sittings with Eusapia Palladino. The sittings were full of attempted tricks on the part of the medium, and in 1894, were declared a failure, not having produced convincing evidence of genuine phenomena. There were good reasons why that series should have failed but they may have had more to do with the personalities involved than with Eusapia: "Eusapia was vital, vulgar, amorous and a cheat, and this combination must have jarred upon those whose interest in psychical research was rather to find a sure road to immortality than to inquire too closely into the queer phenomena produced by a woman whose behaviour both in and out of the cabinet revealed a femininity which must often have been a little disturbing to the Cambridge philosophers." (Dingwall n.d.: 189-90)

Eusapia may have been all of those things but she could also produce, under strict controls, results which remain inexplicable to this day. One "splendid example" quoted by Carrington was the occasion when Carrington took Howard Thurston, then America's most successful magician, to see the medium. Having warned Thurston about Eusapia's love of mischief, they let her know by their manner that they knew when she "tried it on" by lifting the table with one toe, whereupon she smiled, settled down, "and finally produced a series of perfectly magnificent levitations, which so convinced Thurston of their genuineness that he came forward in the papers the next day with a thousand-dollar challenge to any magician who could produce them under the same conditions." (Carrington 1954: 22).

Such a mixture of genuine phenomena and trickery may be a common feature of physical mediumship, but it does offer a way out of having to face up to anything that does not fit in with a worldview which rules out the very possibility of the anomalous. The assumption "once a cheat, always a cheat", apart from being inaccurate and simplistic in its moral rectitude, is also a very effective way of dismissing as worthless a whole body of relevant evidence in general, as well as damaging reputations with long-term consequences. Any claim to explaining the phenomena by "natural" means (i.e., cheating) is much more likely to be taken at face value and not examined further. As recently as 1996, in a preface to his classic work *On Mental Suggestion* (1887), Julian Ochorowicz, otherwise regarded as the father of Polish psychology, was being taken to task for believing in the reality of mediumistic

---

[5] Henry Sidgwick, Professor of Moral Philosophy and his mathematician wife Eleanor, Frederic Myers and Dr Richard Hodgson.

phenomena even though, in "a famous incident with Eusapia Palladino [...] Hugo Münsterberg, in an extremely simple and clever way, proved her to be fraudulent in moving a table with her foot in 1909, and she had been suspected of fraud earlier as well." (Ochorowicz 1996: 7-31)

In fact, Hugo Münsterberg, professor of psychology at Harvard, made up the incident and was accused by Carrington, on the basis of stenographic records and witness evidence, of "willful falsehood". (Sommer 2012; Carrington 1913). This is an extreme case but, in the field of psychical research, there are many more cases where accusations and assumptions of cheating are based on distortion, suppression, and biased selection of facts. A great many explanations, both by academics and amateurs, achieve success by ignoring the full picture. In the words of Ochorowicz after his first series of sittings with Palladino: "It would [...] be safer to omit the stranger portion of facts, and relate the less controversial part of the story in such a manner that the reader would gain a high regard for the author's cleverness in solving the most complex puzzles. [...] One needs only to stretch some facts, drop certain others, here and there round out certain details with assumptions, and end with a tirade against the gullibility of certain scientists. It would then be said that the subject is of interest and very soberly written." (Ochorowicz 1913-15; translated by Casimir Bernard)

Even Kluski, although his mediumship was, basically, a private and personal matter, attracted misplaced and unfounded accusations of refusing to admit a conjurer even though no such request had been made, and of not submitting to examination by unspecified scientific panels. His mediumship became known when Dr Gustave Geley, a French researcher, published accounts of a number of séances with Kluski which were conducted at the Institut Métapsychique International in Paris, and in Warsaw. These accounts contained detailed descriptions of the events which took place, including many phenomena which should be impossible not only under the conditions prevailing at the séances, but simply impossible, such as lights emanating from the medium, turning into faces and figures, floating across the room, touching the sitters, and responding to unspoken requests. Amazing as these events were, it was the production of paraffin moulds of "spirit" hands (Geley's almost obsessive quest for the Permanent Paranormal Object) which attracted, and still attracts, most attention and controversy. The continuing interest in this phenomenon might have something to do with the ease with which one can apply to it Ochorowicz's recipe for scientific success: it is very easy to demonstrate that such moulds can be produced naturally, provided one has the appropriate tools and sufficient time.

It is wrong to put one's theory or beliefs above facts, just as it is wrong not to tell the whole truth, and yet the temptation is quite understandable when faced with facts which defy belief, as is the case with some physical mediumship. We may not know exactly what consciousness is and hold varying views on what it is capable of, but we are familiar with the idea that we can subconsciously respond to stimuli of which we are not aware. We might extend this idea to accept, for example, telepathy, and try to explain it through a variety of theoretical approaches, (for example, in terms of signals, fields or non-locality). Accepting telepathy may strain the worldview for some of us - but not as much as does a third arm grown suddenly to turn off the light that is out of reach!

With Kluski, this is just for starters. And yet, just as with the best of Palladino and a few others, dismissing the recorded evidence would be equivalent to deciding that scores of reputable scientists, experienced investigators well aware of mediumistic tricks, and other people whose judgment one would normally trust without hesitation, must be deeply deficient both intellectually and morally. Julian Ochorowicz hoped to advance science by "telling all", regardless of how impossible it might seem, and so did Hereward Carrington. I add the material on Kluski in the same enquiring spirit which made Ochorowicz ask: What is impossible?

CHAPTER 1

SETTING THE SCENE: SPECIAL TIMES, SPECIAL PEOPLE

Kluski's mediumship developed at a time when what had seemed impossible was coming true on a national scale. After more than a hundred years of being partitioned between the empires of Russia, Prussia and Austria, years which saw a constant and exhausting struggle to preserve national identity, an independent Poland emerged from the aftermath of the First World War on 11 November 1918. The country faced enormous problems in trying to build a new unified state on the ruins of a land ravaged by war and plundered by the departing powers, yet it was also a period of great creativity, optimism, and dynamism, in all aspects of public life: artistic, literary, academic, social, political and economic.

In any nation, the percentage of active freedom fighters will be small. In the case of those who fought for Poland's independence, the most famous and successful were the Legions of Józef Piłsudski, formed in 1914 to fight for Polish independence alongside the Austro-Hungarian army. The Legionists may not have had the military training of professional forces, nor their experience, but they were enthusiastic, courageous, optimistic, resourceful and adaptable. In fact, after experiencing their fighting ability, the German military authorities wanted to create a volunteer Polish army to fight against Russia (Pajewski 1995).

With Piłsudski in a position of great influence after independence was achieved, many of the officers close to him naturally became involved in establishing the new structures of state, legislature and the military, many of them reaching high ranks in their fields. Interestingly, they represent a significant contingent among those who took part in sittings with Kluski - interestingly, because the presence of such individuals may have contributed to the success of these sittings. Many of them not only had the qualities of extraversion and fearlessness which fitted them for leadership, but their wartime stories also bear witness to some of them having a "charmed" life by their ability to make it through life-threatening situations. It is by now accepted that extraversion and a positive attitude aid performance in tests of psychic ability, while the concept of luck may be more complex than is generally believed. It was certainly treated as a pointer to anomalous abilities by the US army when it was choosing potential candidates for their Stargate project (perhaps taking their cue from Napoleon's famous request "Give me lucky generals")[1]. The intuitive, pragmatic, and apparently correct assumption behind the selection process was that the people likely to have something "extra" would be the ones who survived against the odds, and the selectors concentrated on identifying those who "had far fewer casualties from booby traps and ambushes than average" (McMoneagle, 2006: 282).

It has not been possible to establish Kluski's involvement with the military, but there is sufficient evidence to show that he was involved in some way. However, Norbert Okołowicz, his best friend, leader at the majority of the séances, and author of *Reminiscences of sittings with the medium Franek Kluski*, the main source of our information about the sittings, certainly belongs among the "larger-than-life" military and other personalities that clustered around Kluski. Okołowicz (1890-1943), graduate in Fine Arts and a successful artist prior to the First World War, joined the Polish Legions during the war and took part in all the major battles. He was wounded on a number of occasions and quickly rose to the rank of captain.

His exploits, including an attempted escape by car between enemy lines, are a fascinating story in themselves. Accused of treason and rebellion by the Austrians alongside other Legionist ringleaders, he

---

[1] The Stargate Project was aimed at investigating the potential military application of remote viewing (clairvoyance) and functioned from the 1970s to mid-1990s. http://archived.parapsych.org/members/e_c_may.html

was expecting to be executed, even sending his wedding ring back to his wife. During the court case he insisted on speaking Polish, making headlines in the press and making the case last until the end of the Austrian monarchy. At the time of the publication of his book on Kluski (1926) he was a Lieutenant Colonel, working for the military on publication of maps, as well as pursuing his interest in sport (chairing one of Warsaw's sports clubs), folk art and, of course, psychical research.[2]

An even greater "larger-than-life" figure who attended Kluski's séances, and perhaps Okołowicz's comrade-at-arms, was Bolesław Wieniawa-Długoszowski (1881-1942). Having proved himself in the battlefield by quite legendary exploits, he became Józef Piłsudski's closest aide-de-camp. Idolised by his men and beloved by a significant number of ladies, this heroic cavalryman, who also found time to be a doctor of medicine and a fun-loving Bohemian poet, also became a successful politician and diplomat; above all, however, he was "a totally committed patriot who entered the pantheon of great Poles" (Wittlin 1996:cover). In the words of a poet friend on his death, Wieniawa-Długoszowski seemed to be life itself, the magic of everyday life, that part of it which we think ought to be immortal and, during the 1920s, at the height of his creative powers, he seemed to be the personification of that ineffable essence of the joy of life.[3]

Many other distinguished military names could be listed, but other important groups of creative high achievers were also represented among the séance participants and they deserve a mention. The most illustrious representatives of the theatrical profession were probably Leon Schiller (1887-1954) and Arnold Szyfman (1882-1967), both famous theatre directors, dramatists, and theorists, whose contribution to the development of the art of theatre in Poland has made them classics in their field. However, long before that, at the start of their careers, they had a great deal of fun producing a very successful literary-artistic cabaret for which Kluski (before he became Kluski) wrote much of the material. The most famous of the writers and journalists who came to Kluski's séances was probably his colleague from work, Tadeusz Boy-Żeleński (1874-1941), a medical doctor by training who

---

[2] Source: http://karpaccy.pl/pulkownik-norbert-okolowicz

[3] Wieniawa committed suicide in 1942, at the age of sixty, discarding a life of comfort, security and inaction (to which he was being sidelined for political reasons) as fearlessly as he embraced the active life of a fighter.

became an outstanding essayist, drama critic, writer and translator of French classical literature, regarded as one of the most influential figures in Poland between the two world wars.

The list of participants in the Kluski séances reads like a "who's who" of Polish intelligentsia of that time, with top representatives from every important milieu: military, artistic, academic, commercial and political. These were not visits to a show given by a fashionable performer which anyone could attend as a form of entertainment, but visits to a private home in order to observe, and be prepared to give witness to, the most unusual phenomena whose existence then, as now, was generally regarded as impossible, while those witnessing them risked being accused of questionable judgment and faulty powers of observation. The reports quoted by Okołowicz in his book were published contemporaneously, including the names of the participants, many of whom also provided signed witness statements.

A significant number of these participants were people who had risked their lives for their principles and for a cause they believed in; people who outwitted or defeated enemies in real-life situations, where the ability to tell the real from the imagined meant life or death; people who had faced death, had seen death all around them, and had come through strong enough to engage fully and with gusto with life on this plane. Yet if we reject the evidence, (which they did their best to produce objectively) we must judge them to be either so lacking in spiritual strength, so fearful of death[4], and so desperate to believe that they never questioned their experience, or to be too feeble-minded to know when they were being deceived.

Even though the 1920s were quite favourable to psychical research and engaging with the subject did not necessarily carry a stigma, this conundrum remains. It is a fact that psychical research was establishing itself as a science, both in the Western world and in Poland. At that time, the French *Institut Métapsychique International*, with Charles Richet and Gustave Geley as its most prominent representatives, served as a model for the Polish psychical researchers, among whom were to be found many academics. Józef Piłsudski, the head of state, was both interested in the subject and reported to have had a

---

[4] Some participants feared that the sittings might be a sin, since the Roman Catholic Church frowns on such activities, and for many of them – including Kluski and Okołowicz, both staunch Catholics - belonging to the church would be an unquestioned part of their national identity.

number of psychic experiences. These circumstances helped to make the subject socially acceptable, but they also helped to spread knowledge about the subject, awareness of the fraudulent tricks, of the need for designing good experiments and for ensuring good controls, in fact, for doing all the things which the participants conscientiously tried to do in the Kluski séances.

And so, we come to the psychical researchers who attended these séances. In fact, Okołowicz himself was very knowledgeable about the subject, aware of the importance of controls, and usually meticulous in his reporting. So were the members of the Polish equivalent of the Society for Psychical Research known to have attended the séances, but some of them may have also contributed to the sittings in ways other than by establishing controls. Of particular interest here is Prosper Szmurło, who worked as a tax inspector but was also very active in psychical research. During the 1920s he chaired the Warsaw Psychophysical Society, and for a number of years edited *Zagadnienia Metapsychiczne (Metapsychical Issues)*, a journal devoted to psychical research. One wonders how much of the successful experimentation obtained by the Society was due to the presence of experimenters such as Szmurło, who himself obtained striking results in the telepathic experiments which took place in 1928. These were arranged by Szmurło and Angelos Tanagras, president of the Greek society, and involved groups of participants in Warsaw and Athens "sending" and "receiving" targets (mainly drawings) by concentrating for fixed periods at specific times. The experiments were reported and analysed in *Zagadnienia Metapsychiczne* in December 1928 and 1929[5]. The results as a whole are impressive, but it is Szmurło (involved in so many investigations, including some of the Kluski sittings[6]), that deserves special attention.

---

[5] Stefan Rzewuski (1928): Results of group telepathic experiments between Athens and Warsaw. *Zagadnienia metapsychiczne* 19-20, 1928, 36-51. Prosper Szmurło (1929): On experiments in telepathy between Athens and Warsaw. *Zagadnienia Metapsychiczne* 23-24, 1929, 21-35 [All translations from Polish are by the author unless stated otherwise]

[6] Okołowicz lists all the names of participants for what he calls "official" séances, but not for the more spontaneous ones. However, we have at least one full report written by Szmurło.

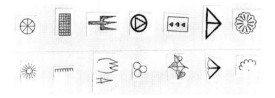

Figure 1: *A sample of the more successful drawings by Prosper Szmurło of the targets "sent" by the team from Athens. The "targets" are shown above Szmurło's corresponding drawings. According to the published calculations, he achieved at least partial success in 10% of his responses; even so, his results were not the best in the Polish team.*

Another member (Vice President) of the Polish Society for Psychical Research whose name appears in the lists of participants in Kluski's séances and who achieved striking successes as an auditive medium (again in a purely private capacity) was Maria Przybylska. Piotr Lebiedziński, another highly respected Polish researcher, presented a paper quoting examples of her clairvoyance and precognition at the Third International Congress of Psychical Research in Paris in 1927 (Lebiedziński, 1928). And, on a number of occasions, Stefan Ossowiecki, perhaps the greatest clairvoyant of them all, attended the sittings as well.

Altogether Kluski's mediumship was witnessed by something like 350 people. Among this number, apart from assorted professors, doctors, lawyers, bankers, industrialists, military men, writers, journalists, artists, and Polish psychical researchers, there were also respected foreign psychical investigators, including Gustave Geley, Charles Richet, Everard Feilding, Camille Flammarion, and Barbara and Hewat McKenzie. The main feature of the testimony left by many of these people is a sense of such genuine wonder at an encounter with a magical world, that it is unlikely to have been achieved using small-scale tricks and sleights of hand. According to Okołowicz, everyone who came to Kluski's séances, including the most adamant sceptics, went away fully convinced of the reality of the phenomena they witnessed. In a book published in 1993 (Bugaj, 1993: 204), Polish researcher Doctor Roman Bugaj reports that he interviewed five of the participants in Kluski's séances, among them Prosper Szmurło, the widow of Norbert Okołowicz, and Tadeusz Urbański[7], and claims that they remained totally

---

[7] Tadeusz Urbański (1901- 1985) was a professor of chemistry who worked at the Military Analytical Laboratory during the years 1922-24. Jan Modrzejewski,

convinced of the genuineness of the phenomena produced during the séances; most regrettably, lack of space prevents him giving any details.

We thus have a private circle with a medium who is on equal terms with a large number of friends and acquaintances, all of them deeply interested in the phenomena which form around him. They are highly educated, creative and observant sitters, and some of them attend quite regularly. The quality of the sitters is reflected in the quality of the reporting. While the majority of the available accounts are collated by Okołowicz, there are also quite a few produced independently by other sitters (as well as in other locations) and, in general, they demonstrate a most commendable detachment, analytical skills, attention to detail, and a critical approach to one's own reactions. If we do not reject them out of hand on the grounds that what they describe could not have happened, then we are forced to come back to the question: what is impossible?

Kluski's son, was his colleague and invited him to a séance with his father. Urbański described his positive impressions in a note in his scientific autobiography published in 1984 (Urbański, 1984: 7-8).

CHAPTER 2

KLUSKI THE PERSON

2.1. Teofil Modrzejewski/Franek Kluski

The pseudonym of Franek Kluski hides a complex and private individual, and the choice of pseudonym itself provides a clue to his ambivalent attitude to the strange gift he possessed. Kluski's real name was Teofil Modrzejewski. In his "mainstream" life he was a banking professional and a creative writer, a family man with a busy and happy life, and a large circle of friends acquired during a varied and successful career. He never performed publicly as a medium, never made any public references to his mediumship, never profited financially from it, and gave it up after a fairly brief period of intense experimentation.

In Polish, both his real first name and surname, Teofil Modrzejewski, sound very respectable but, on the other hand, Franek Kluski, the pseudonym under which he is known as a medium, is less than commonplace: "kluski" in Polish refers to a somewhat dull type of pasta, and the name conveys an image of someone clumsy and dull ("ciepłe kluski" - "warmed-up pasta" can be used to describe someone totally lacking in charisma).

Teofil Modrzejewski was born on 13 February 1873 into a middle class family who lived in Warsaw, where Teofil went to school. Details of his academic achievements and early days are sparse but, according to the Polish Biographical Dictionary and evidence from contemporaries, his main profession was banking, and by the 1920s he was on the board of one of the main banks in Warsaw (Bank Rotwanda). He was also active as a journalist, a poet, and a writer. His career as a medium (but never a public one) began in 1918 and lasted a number of years, with an interruption during the Russian-Polish war in 1920, in which he took part as a volunteer. We cannot be certain when he gave up physical mediumship altogether, but he did become less active in that area from 1925 onwards, mainly because the experiments had an adverse effect on his health. He was married and had at least one son and one daughter. He died of tuberculosis on 22 January 1943 in Warsaw and is buried there. His obituary was signed by his daughter and sisters.

Mediumistic activity, important as it was to him as a personal and private sphere of his life, was not an area in which he tried to make an impression on the world. In fact, it does not fit in very well with his personality as revealed away from séances, and he was not convinced that popularising such phenomena was a good thing. He did achieve a brief period of notoriety as a medium (it is doubtful whether he would have called it fame), but by profession he was a man of letters. Everything that we know about him as a person points to the conclusion that it is in that capacity that he would have preferred to make his mark. As it happens, he did make enough of an impression as a writer to have earned himself a very small but respectable position on the Warsaw literary scene of the early 20th century but, by and large, his work survives now in library archives rather than in the public mind. Preferring his literary work to stand on its own merit, he never wrote about his mediumistic experiences, fearing the kind of sensationalism they would attract, and although he allowed researchers to investigate the phenomena he produced, he never tried to obtain any material benefit from his psychic abilities. He was offered large sums of money to undertake tours of America but, as he confided to a contemporary, he believed that he could not convince the whole world that he was not cheating, and therefore would rather leave his children a name unsullied by controversy.

2.2. Early years, living and writing

According to Geley, the French psychical researcher who investigated Kluski when he was about fifty, Franek Kluski was extremely impressionable and emotional, very likeable, highly congenial, intelligent, very well educated, and a polyglot. He agreed to take part in the experiments for no fee and, at that time, had been practising mediumship for about 18 months. His psychic gifts were probably inherited from his father who, although he never gave séances, found spontaneous phenomena constantly happening in his presence. Kluski had clear recollections of such episodes. His paternal uncle, a Catholic priest, also had mediumistic faculties, and frequently had veridical telepathic visions.

Franek's childhood was thus full of marvellous accounts of paranormal experiences and these made all the more impression on him as his health was very delicate. It seems that some of his siblings died at an early age, and he himself suffered a number of serious illnesses as a child, which would perhaps account in part for his being dreamy and contemplative.

At that time he was subject to presentiments, had exact visions of events at a distance, and perceived "phantoms", which to him appeared to be living. At the age of 5-6 these visions became particularly clear and frequent. He found them perfectly natural and neither feared them nor found them strange. He talked to them familiarly and found them welcoming and friendly.

Many sources confirm that Kluski would not talk about his personal views regarding his gift and would usually avoid the subject by turning it into a joke. When the mood was right and the company congenial, his wife and children would apparently talk about various episodes from Kluski's life, but apart from a few anecdotes quoted in the book by his friend Okołowicz, none of them have been made public. The only direct information we have about the early experiences is what Kluski wrote for Geley, who published it in his *L'Ectoplasmie et La Clairvoyance*. It is perhaps testimony to Geley's sensitive approach that Kluski, so reluctant to reveal his feelings on the subject, provided Geley with a glimpse of his childhood experiences. The story reads like a literary piece, and it is difficult to tell how far it is accurate or metaphorical, but on that unique occasion it seems that the person speaking is Teofil Modrzejewski rather than Kluski, and the writing rings with personal sentiment and genuine background detail.

Referring to himself in the third person as 'the little boy', Kluski describes a secret game which consisted in going to see 'the mole'. This involved crawling into a tent made out of chairs covered with a shawl, and the story given to Geley is woven around an evening when the parents are out and the little boy invites other children, together with their "little nursemaid", to the tent. In Kluski's own words:

Outside it was freezing hard. The room was heated by a large porcelain stove, which then gave out sharp crackling sounds. The nursemaid, thinking that the stove had been overheated, wanted to open the door, but as the crackling became louder she was afraid and remained still. The children, too, were afraid to move. The little boy then rose, went out of the tent towards the stove. At that moment the lamp went out, and from out the door of the stove there came a blue mist, which surrounded the boy and floated out into the room. The children cried out in fear, but the little boy told them not to be afraid; it was just the mole coming. He got them all together under the tent to tell them the story of the mole. His voice had changed. It said that the road to the mole was a very long one; it goes through long, dark passages, and one must wait till the darkness passes; it then becomes brighter.

He said that when little children die they are buried because they can then get at the mole more easily. He advised the children to be very quiet and good, so as to get to the mole without frightening it. ... "Although the room was in darkness, the inside of the tent was lit with a dim light, and the children saw, to their amazement, a little brother and sister who had died. They understood that these were going to the mole's kingdom, and were more astonished than afraid.

The figures of the dead children faded little by little, and the children begged the little boy to go on with the journey to the mole. He told them that this was impossible, but he showed them a small luminous fissure, and told them to look through it. Before their eyes there unrolled a number of rooms and passages, lit as with gems. The rooms were full of human forms, transparent and bright, floating in the air [...]

But the landscapes began to get vague, and a gust of wind seemed to blow away the rooms and the people, and then all vanished. (Geley 1927: 200-204)

The parents returned from the theatre, the children and the nursemaid were reprimanded for staying up late, but the little boy did not care because he knew he could rejoin the mole when he was alone by leaving his body. After initial difficulties, he learned to do this habitually at night. There follow descriptions of premonitions: one is an incident in which during an out-of-body experience he visits an unfamiliar house and sees his mother ill, with a horrible apparition called 'pneumonia' by her bed. In the summer the family goes to the country and mother falls ill with pneumonia.

Gradually the journeys to the mole became less frequent and eventually ceased altogether. However, he would see "phantoms" of deceased relations and friends, as well as animals, around him when he was in the open and at night in bed, and they were always friendly. These visions increased at the time of puberty. When he was sixteen he fell in love with a girl who died. This was a traumatic event which left a permanent mark on his mind and was followed by various visions of her.

Very little personal information on Kluski is available for the period when he was most active professionally. Geley and Okołowicz tell us that from the age of 20 until he was 46 Kluski was busy with ordinary life, working, getting married, bringing up children, and not paying much attention to his visions[1]. (Rare glimpses of his private life indicate a happy family). Yet a number of confirmed extraordinary events did take place during that time. One of them was the duel Kluski fought at the age of 27, in about 1900. According to Okołowicz, the scar where the bullet entered was at the level of the fourth rib, pushing the nipple slightly inward. It lodged in Kluski's chest and, by the time of the "radiogram" reported by Geley, it had slipped downwards and outwards to the level of the tenth rib. By the time he met Geley, Kluski was in the habit of recounting his duelling adventure as a humorous story, which included the surgeon's amazement at a patient regarded as dead coming back to life. It is hard to say whether this traumatic incident had any other repercussions apart from the violent heart palpitations from which Kluski suffered from then on, yet this is another feature which makes him just that much more different from most people.

Another development which must have been formative was Modrzejewski's involvement with writing for the popular stage during the years 1909-1912. We do not know how he came to join the team which wrote for "Momus", a Warsaw literary-artistic cabaret, but we do know, from sources totally unconnected with psychical research, that he enjoyed great success in this area. While the term "cabaret" may immediately bring to mind images of burlesque and dancing girls, at that

---

[1] However, he must have also been remarkably successful in his professional life. The family lived in one of the most attractive and prestigious buildings in Warsaw (Królewska 16), built in 1881, with a fashionable restaurant on the ground floor, and, interestingly, the editorial office of the "Freethinker", an atheist publication, on the first floor. (Kledzik, 2003)

time this form of popular entertainment often carried ambitious and sophisticated content (of course, alongside the dancing girls!). Based on the Parisian and German models, it was a commercial enterprise with artistic ambitions. It made a living by challenging the bourgeois values of the very bourgeois who came to enjoy being abused by the fascinating boheme. The cabaret became so popular that it soon had to move to larger premises. The topicality, as well as the sheer wit and artistic quality of the programmes, attracted Warsaw elites and tickets were hard to get. Reviews warmly praised the young and un-inhibited authors who seemed to know instinctively how to use the freedom offered by the "cabaret muse" to bring important issues to public attention and to make people feel and think. From the very first performance, Modrzejewski's contributions became one of the main attractions of Momus, and his name came at the top amongst the au-thors when advertising a new premiere. His poetry was very versat-ile, from seriously patriotic through fervent social and political satire, humorous or frivolous mini-dramas and "stage pictures", to comic or sentimental songs, some of which became such popular "hits" that, in time, they came to be regarded as anonymous creations of the urban folklore of Warsaw. At the same time, one of the most highly praised satires on the current political situation was Modrzejewski's "Un-Divine Comedy", a journey through the Dantean hell in which the audience could easily recognise the Tsarist Duma - that parody of a parliament - and the Polish Circle which functioned within it (Karwacka 1982).[2] His social satires, seething with indignation against various examples of injustice, inequality, and hypocrisy, demonstrate a similar breadth of knowledge and awareness of wider social issues, but also expressed in easy, popular verses. A writer reveals himself to a certain extent in his work: most of Kluski's poetry shows real concern, but the expres-sion is always flippant. To give an example, in one poem he describes, in exactly the same language, a rich girl frustrated with a boring hol-iday, and a poor girl desperately looking for work. Their ensuing fate (the rich girl finding a lover, and the poor girl committing suicide) are ascribed to the same cause, lack of gainful employment. This flippant approach can be very effective, but it is also limiting, and it could be ar-gued that Kluski was too sensitive, too private a person, to achieve true self-expression as an artist, hence his career turned towards journalism rather than literature. From the accounts of the séances, which make

[2] Warsaw was within the Polish partition under Russian rule.

it clear that Kluski worked both during the day and at night (fitting in the séances in late evening), it seems likely that journalism was an adjunct to his work at the bank. By the beginning of the twentieth century he was the economic correspondent of one of the Warsaw dailies (*Kurier Poranny*). Over the next quarter of the century he had, on and off, his own column there, and throughout his active professional life he contributed occasional verses, often satirical, to a variety of periodicals and anthologies. He also translated a novel from Italian, and in the 1930s published a volume of linguistic research on *Words which have died and are dying*. This work reveals him as a linguistic purist and a patriot, arguing for the preservation of old Polish words, against borrowing loanwords from non-Slavonic languages, and for returning to Slavonic roots.

The Polish Biographical Dictionary lists the dates and the periodicals in which Modrzejewski's contributions appeared. All the entries either pre-date or post-date the Great War of 1914-1918. So far, I have not been able to establish what happened to Modrzejewski and his family during that period. Poland, partitioned between Russia, Germany and Prussia at the end of the eighteenth century, with millions of Poles conscripted into their armies in 1914, served as a battlefield for the warring sides, with the German army taking Warsaw from Russia in 1915 and occupying it until 1918. As the war developed, both Russia and Germany tried to attract Polish support with promises of greater independence, while a number of Polish factions struggled towards regaining an independent country both through political and military means, forming various strategic alliances.

Considering the intense patriotism of his poetry and his absence from the literary scene, it is most likely that Modrzejewski would have been involved in that struggle in some way. We do have information that he was accepted as a volunteer for the Polish army, as an officer in a dragoon regiment, in 1920 (Sokołowski, 1936), which suggests previous experience and contacts. Perhaps most tellingly, as has been mentioned already, many of the participants in the séances of the 1920s are high-ranking military men and politicians who came to power upon Poland achieving independence on 11 November 1918.

On the other hand, Kluski's association with people such as Arnold Szyfman and Leon Schiller, (great names in the history of Polish theatre) goes back to his "cabaret" days. Kluski's séances were private, almost in the nature of a home circle, and certainly did not in any way resemble the public performances described in literature on physical mediumship. The character and the diversity of the participants re-flects the range of Modrzejewski's interests and connections with the world of the artistic, military, and political elite, as well as his ability to form and maintain lasting friendships (Okołowicz comments on the fact that people tended to like Kluski very much, as did animals). But the very fact of holding séances also reflects, apart from his interest in mediumship, perhaps also an interest in dramatic performance. This is not a hint of possible fraud, but rather speculation that an aspect of his personality, which perhaps had little chance of expressing itself in his middle age, suddenly found an outlet. A convincing case could be made for the claim that the diverse characteristics of the phantoms which appeared at the séances reflect to some extent the dichotomy in Kluski's nature: too sensitive and too private to reveal what his gift really meant to him, a trait which also led him to escape into flippancy or "public" attitudes in his writing.

2.3. Life with mediumship

The two detailed sources relating to Kluski's mediumship, by Geley and Okołowicz, also offer revealing glimpses of his private life. While Geley provides a unique reminiscence of Kluski's childhood, the volume by Okołowicz (probably Kluski's closest friend) offers much greater detail and covers the period of Kluski's involvement in mediumship (1918-1925). Tantalisingly, he tells us that he has enough material for another book, and also that he omits many important details because they are too personal.

Both Geley and Okołowicz provide summaries of Kluski's physical condition, again more detailed in the case of Okołowicz who, apart from being able to observe the medium more closely and for longer, also includes opinions from physicians other than Geley who examined Kluski on a variety of occasions.

At the time when Geley carried out his experiments with Kluski in Paris (1920), Kluski was 47 years old. Geley describes him as delic-ate but in good health with no organic defects, thin and of medium height, and draws attention to Kluski's "hyper-excitable nervous sys-tem, physical and mental", which makes him impressionable and emo-tional. Kluski was often seriously ill as a child and, according to Geley, all of his siblings had died, but this may have been a misunderstand-ing, since Kluski's obituary was signed by his sisters.

Okołowicz tells us that Kluski was exceptional in many ways, including the strange nature of his numerous serious illnesses. He would fall ill suddenly, with the illness reaching its crisis within a few hours. However, in a short while the fever would suddenly abate and Kluski would get up and start normal work again. Sometimes he would be in perfect health but within a few hours only to fall ill again with another grave illness without the usual initial symptoms. These extreme and violent swings in his physical health would be matched by swings in his mental and emotional state. A clue to the nature of these illnesses may be provided by the fact that Kluski's physical state would more often than not improve suddenly with the improvement of his emotional state, and during times of depression, physical problems would also appear immediately.

Okołowicz describes Kluski's everyday life as very different from that of the average person. The medium's enormous sensitivity, with frequent changes of mental state from confusion to total clarity, could be disconcerting even to those who were nearest and dearest to him.

Generally, he would come alive only in the evening, working during the day in a somewhat apathetic, mechanistic manner. Most of his activity, not just as a medium but as a poet and journalist, took place at night. This started from his earliest youth, when he was forced to work at night over and above the day's work. He had the ability to sleep for about 3 hours in 24 and feel as rested as others would after a full night's sleep.

In spite of his sensitivity and fluctuating health, Kluski is described as being a practical person with his feet on the ground, and he was not given to mysticism. He is certainly reported to have been fond of risqué jokes and some of his verses bear this out. Some of his comments indicate that he looked down on what he termed the "circus" of mediumship and he lacked any ambition to establish himself as a medium whilst being genuinely interested in psychical research. His level of education and intelligence meant that, while being open to suggestions, especially regarding details of the séances, he would follow his own convictions and not deviate from them. Hence his refusal to use his mediumship to make his journalism popular, to talk about the subject, or to give explanations, which he was often asked to do. While he cooperated closely with Polish psychical researchers and tried not to refuse the requests of foreign ones (holding séances even when under pressure of poor health and professional commitments), Kluski did not seek out investigators. The only exception was his visit to IMI, but this

was done as a favour during a trip to Paris which was totally unconnected with psychical research. Okołowicz makes the point of refut-
ing the accusation made against Kluski by the French journalist Paul
Heuzé who, in his book *Do the dead live?* claimed that Kluski would
not agree to take part in a séance with a magician named Dickson, or
some other conjurer. This was totally false, since nobody named Dickson, nor any other conjurer, ever approached Kluski. It was not the only
slur on Modrzejewski's good name, since in his *Fifty Years of Psychical
Research* Harry Price also implies that there was something suspicious
in his being unable to obtain sittings with Kluski during his two visits
to Warsaw and in Kluski never having "submitted himself to a scientific panel" (Price 1939: 28). Clearly, Price did not understand how the
Kluski séances worked: while Geley and Richet, both courteous and
supportive, had an excellent relationship with the Polish researchers
and hence a way into what was essentially a 'home circle', a stranger
demanding entry would naturally be rebuffed. It would be a different
story with friends or friends of friends. For example, on 29 April 1923,
Kluski, in spite of being poorly and extremely overworked, held a séance
for Professor Henri Breuil, the famous French anthropologist, because
Breuil had a letter of recommendation from Geley. Like the true gentleman that he was, when faced with people desperate after the loss of
their loved ones (who would have found their way to him via friends,
or friends of friends), Kluski would always give them priority regardless of their status. He would not do this for gain but would offer them
hospitality in his own time at his own home.

Yet his involvement with physical mediumship cost him a lot of suffering and his health problems seemed to worsen, as if perfecting his
mediumship went hand in hand with a worsening physical condition.
Sometimes, the day after a séance, bleeding and wounds appeared, only
to disappear without trace after a day or two, and his body would emanate the scent of ozone. He suffered from tachycardia, palpitations,
extreme fatigue, fainting fits, catalepsy, internal and external bleeding,
vomiting, and intestinal troubles. After his return from Paris, where
he experimented with Geley in 1920, Kluski's health deteriorated significantly. He became apathetic and unsociable, with frequent fainting fits. He began to be revolted by the séances and forced himself to
carry them out, at the same time seeming not to be interested in the
phenomena. His previous active mediumship gave way to passivity.
His digestive trouble gradually worsened and the last series of séances
caused persistent vomiting. His perseverance in holding séances under

these circumstances might thus be seen as a kind of compulsion, addiction, or the fulfilment of an obligation, especially as we are told that months could go by without them and he would then feel and look a lot better, be less agitated, and even need more sleep.

Kluski's ambivalent attitude to his gift was probably also affected by his religious feelings. Okołowicz describes him as a deeply religious Catholic, concerned that the séances might provide grounds for the rise of a religious doctrine. The later sittings provide evidence of Kluski's Christian beliefs through the powerful spiritual and religious imagery of the phantoms produced. The Catholic church, however, was firmly opposed to displays of mediumistic abilities regardless of their content. Although occasional physical séances may have continued for a while after the publication of the book by Okołowicz in 1926, later mediumship seems to have mainly involved automatic writing. However, in an unpublished manuscript, Antoni Czubryński (Czubryński: 1934-1946), a psychical researcher, reports indignantly that at the outbreak of the Second World War in September 1939, Kluski, anxious like millions of others, went to confession and was told to cease his mediumistic activities (by then probably mainly automatic writing), which he did immediately.

2.4. Living with phantoms

While most of Kluski's characteristics described so far may be unusual or extreme, they are not beyond the range of human experience as we know it. However, the phenomena which we are about to encounter now seem to belong to another realm, even though, according to Okołowicz and other witnesses, they happened outside the séances and seemed also to be part of Kluski's everyday life. For this reason, as well as because they are purely anecdotal in not being included in formal reports signed by witnesses, they are included here rather than as part of his mediumistic phenomena.

The most common of these would be knockings from various items of furniture, sometimes weaker and sometimes stronger. They did not seem to be mindless but appeared to be more in the nature of positive or negative responses to a conversation being carried on somewhere, perhaps just in someone's mind. They were usually single but more rarely double or triple knocks. Their effect on the medium would be that of light pain and a shock, appearing without Kluski's conscious involvement, and they would annoy him by interrupting his work as if trying to intrude or to draw attention to themselves. Kluski's apartment would also often be full of noises which resembled furniture being moved, or steps, or rustling of papers. When the residents looked for their source, the noises would disappear from the room which was being searched and move to the one which had just been searched. Such effects would appear more often and more clearly in periods of intense séancing, particularly before and after séances. Less frequent were such things as hitting the keys of the piano (even when closed) and, during one period, there was knocking on the outside of the window panes (Kluski's apartment being on the fourth floor). Papers would be moved, and typewriter keys would type by themselves. Sometimes very fast, faultless messages would appear on the typewriter, typed in Polish but sometimes in Italian. They would be typed in the dark and faster and better than the medium would be able to type. This might also happen in full light and even in the medium's absence, or the typewriter would carry on typing if Kluski interrupted work and moved away. Sometimes the knocking noises would start up in apartments where Kluski was a more frequent visitor, sometimes after he left and often just before he arrived.

The light phenomena were also quite common outside the séances. They would be little lights, very useful on some occasions, such as when going down unlit stairs. This phenomenon, confirmed by witnesses, would take the form of a small green light floating in front of Kluski, about 50 cm from his face. The light would go up and down depending on whether one had to lift or lower the foot at the end or beginning of the steps. The light would float calmly along a horizontal line between obstacles, and when one needed to turn, it would turn first in the appropriate direction. Yet it did not seem to be something that Kluski willed to happen. His attitude was that "life belongs to the living" and he was unwilling to rely on "other-worldly" assistance. Light hazes were often seen around him, and sometimes little fires inside his mouth. A businessman who unexpectedly had to share a hotel room with Kluski noticed the light phenomena and strange noises while Kluski was asleep. Light spots were also observed on the medium outside the trance state when he was deeply moved about something. Okołowicz also records an incident in Vienna, when he and Kluski went into an optician's shop to have broken glasses repaired and had to leave in a hurry when all the needles in a display of compasses under the glass counter went haywire after Kluski leaned across it.

A feature reported by a number of witnesses is the frequent turning on and off of electrical lights outside séances. A friend and work colleague jokingly reports that they always knew when Kluski came to work in the editorial office, since lights would begin to flicker and become unreliable. There are also reports of how Kluski reacted to an impending storm and during it. Okołowicz describes him becoming very agitated, his limbs hot, something like an electrical discharge going through his body. It manifested itself by the tingling and stiffening of toes and particularly fingers, with bluish flames escaping at times from the ends of his fingers, something which could be seen in a darkened room. A storm seemed to exhaust him in a way similar to a séance, and he would be adamant about not holding a séance at such time.

Odours are another phenomenon particularly commented on by everyone writing about Kluski. His colleagues at the bank related that after Modrzejewski walked down an acacia-lined avenue, they were unable to stay in the same room with him because he reeked of the plant. The most frequent and characteristic was the smell of ozone, referred to in most accounts of the séances, but it seemed to stay with him long afterwards, sometimes as much as two days, permeating everything associated with him: his apartment, his clothes, his whole body. The same applied to things he ingested or came into contact with, such as alcohol or flowers. The smells produced during the séances: disease, animals, flowers, etc., would also cling to him for a long time.

There are other examples of this strange ability to absorb or act like a conductor. After a séance, in June 1919, Kluski felt very weak and asked Dr Tadeusz Sokołowski (a prominent psychical researcher) for some magnetic passes to help him recover and carry on with his work. Dr Sokołowski, who had come directly from a dinner, did as requested and on leaving asked to be telephoned if things got worse. A few minutes later Kluski became dizzy and vomited, showing all the signs of alcohol poisoning which was strange, as he had not drunk any alcohol in the preceding few days. A little later Dr Sokołowski telephoned to say that immediately after leaving Kluski he felt much better, even though after the meal, during which he drank alcohol, he felt dizzy and had a bit of a stomach upset. He added that while he was magnetising Kluski he noticed purple flashes coming out of Kluski's fingers, such as those he had noticed during experiments with magnets.

We are also told that on a number of occasions people close to Kluski observed his misty figure in their apartments in the evening or at night. These appearances were brief, and one could communicate with them only sometimes in a whisper or by knocking. Generally they seemed misty and flowing, yet at times not different from a living person. Sometimes these phantoms would disperse quickly and the places from which they disappeared would emit knockings. In such cases the friends would almost always telephone Kluski at home, usually waking him from sleep. This was possible when Kluski was in Warsaw, but such appearances could also happen at a greater distance. In November 1920, Dr Geley saw Kluski close to his old apartment in Paris at a time when Kluski was in Warsaw, which was proved by checking his passport. When asked, Kluski admitted that he could travel like that consciously.

Before Kluski started to hold séances, he experienced clairvoyance. At times he would see multicoloured streaks of light around people's heads and shoulders, and even consulted doctors about it worried that it might be an eye disease, but no disease was found. Such experiences became stronger at the beginning of 1920, coinciding with his séance activities and, even though he was not familiar with the literature of the subject, he realised what was happening when he found that he could describe a person's emotional and mental state, despite being shortsighted and unable to distinguish people at a distance. His experience seems to correspond to that of Stefan Ossowiecki, but Kluski did not try to develop this ability.

Perhaps the strangest thing about Kluski is not so much the claims of his bilocation or clairvoyance but the strange cloud of "presences" with which he seemed to exist. Apparently, throughout his life he had never felt alone; even when far from family and from people, he always had the impression of some life close by which would constantly remind him of its existence. Taking issue with Geley's claim that while experiments cannot take place without the medium, a medium left to itself is helpless, Okołowicz says that this cannot apply to Kluski, whose phenomena took place independently and outside the séance room. Often people would enter his room and would find him lying down surrounded by luminous mists and lights which would start to disappear, possibly because of the presence of visitors. On a number of occasions friends calling on Kluski would peer in to make sure he was not asleep, knowing that he often worked throughout the night and how important it was for him to catch up with his rest when he could, and sometimes phantoms would be seen moving around with the medium among them.

Although this had been going on for over 20 years, the family continued to find it unnerving because of the impression that there were living entities around. On a number of occasions outside the séances, whispers and voices could be heard, directed either at all those present or at individuals. At times there would be a sudden outburst of the smell of ozone, incense, gumtree, or other smells. These "presences" could, however, be extremely helpful. Okołowicz recounts an event for which there was another witness, a medical doctor, Dr Guirard. Kluski was complaining of a toothache which was stopping him from working. He showed to Okołowicz and Dr Guirard a very rotten tooth surrounded by inflammation in his mouth. Guirard regretted that he had not got his instruments with him to remove it, but then he and Okołowicz were called away to tea in another room, and Kluski, suffering badly, lay down again on the settee. When the doctor and Okołowicz returned to the room some 15 minutes later, Kluski was asleep. When he woke up and the light was turned on, they all saw that very tooth with a bloody root on the table next to him. When they looked at the cavity left behind the doctor was very surprised, because under normal conditions a tooth decayed to that extent could not be removed without more damage and bleeding to the gum. Both the doctor and Okołowicz were certain that nobody had entered the room while they were absent.

Dr Sokołowski relates an incident recounted to him by Kluski which again points to his receiving help from some unusual source. As a volunteer in a dragoon regiment, Kluski had to take part in a feast given by the officers in honour of a delegation from another regiment, which included a number of Tartars. After a meal generously supplemented by drink, Kluski, somewhat merry, sat down next to the Tartars and had a lively conversation with them. The next day Kluski's immediate superior expressed his surprise at Kluski's excellent knowledge of the Tartar language, which had amazed the Tartar officers. Kluski, equally amazed, admitted to having had a conversation but observed that he did not know the Tartar language at all. All the officers, one of whom had studied Oriental languages, protested that Kluski did know it. They remembered perfectly how even the regiment's leader remarked that it was somewhat tactless for the group which Kluski had joined to speak a language which was incomprehensible to the rest of the company. (Sokołowski 1936: 101-103).

However, on another occasion the annoyed "presences" played a nasty trick on him. Kluski had to copy dozens of leaflets and, having done so, he left them rolled up for a couple of hours while he went out. When he came back, he found to his horror that every leaflet had written across it "how easy it is to destroy the fruit of human labour".

Kluski was not amused, but remembered that when he was editing the leaflets originally, the typewriter kept typing by itself and, irritated, he berated the phantoms aloud for their unwanted efforts to help.

Unfortunately, we will never know what Kluski's own experience of his gift really was, but it sounds as if the relationship between 'the little boy' and 'the mole' from the story recounted to Geley developed and stayed close throughout the boy's adult life.

CHAPTER 3

SÉANCES AND PHENOMENA

3.1. Development of mediumship

The main body of evidence of Kluski's mediumship is provided by the book *Reminiscences of Séances with the Medium Franek Kluski*, published in Polish in Warsaw in 1926, and consisting of 586 pages supplemented by photographs and drawings. That volume also includes most of the material published by Gustave Geley in his *L'Ectoplasmie et La Clairvoyance* and as articles in *Revue Metapsychique*, translated into Polish and describing the séances held under laboratory conditions at IMI in Paris. Okołowicz's book was authorised by Kluski, and its author was, in his own words, Kluski's best friend, able to observe him in much of everyday life. The main purpose of the book was to make public the factual evidence relating to the séances, concentrating on detailed reports of individual sittings, but it also provides a very general classification of the phenomena and a discussion of how events during the séances might be influenced by the conditions under which they were held.

The reports are based on the testimonies of the participants, often including accounts of the events during the séances and also impressions of the witnesses obtained during the discussions and interviews which followed. Much of the material involved input from members of the Polish equivalent of the Society for Psychical Research in Warsaw, as well as from a number of experienced foreign researchers (mainly Gustave Geley and Charles Richet, with occasional witnesses such as Camille Flammarion, Karl Vett or Everard Feilding). All the reported séances had a system of controls, and those employed at the "official" ones are usually described in detail. However, bearing in mind the relationship between Kluski and his sitters, there were also many impromptu sittings or simply anomalous events which cannot be ignored.

According to Okołowicz, Kluski's career as a medium began at the end of 1918 when he was invited to a test séance with the medium N. (Jan Guzik, according to some sources), who was supposed to be the source of very strong phenomena. These experiments took place under the leadership of Dr Tadeusz Sokołowski, President of the Polish Society for Psychical Research at that time. The séance in which Kluski participated was the fifth in a series, with no phenomena appearing in any of the previous ones. Apart from the host, the medium, Dr Sokołowski, and Kluski, there were three other persons present. Shortly after the light was turned off rustles and knocks could be heard and touches could be felt, not near the medium, but near Kluski. After the séance there was a discussion as to who actually was the medium, and it was decided that it was probably one of the participants, Miss W., who, like Kluski, attended a séance for the first time and was very agitated as the phenomena developed. A week later a séance was held under the same conditions, but without Miss W. who did not come in spite of having promised to do so. The phenomena were much stronger than at the previous séance, and clustered mainly around Kluski. After the séance it was noticed that his eyes had a strange expression, as if of a person woken from somnambulic sleep.

A few days later Kluski visited Dr Sokołowski and talked to him about metapsychical phenomena. The doctor mentioned that some sensitives can sometimes see coloured rays from different objects. Kluski became interested and so they conducted some experiments. When Kluski held a large magnet there were purple flashes from the poles, and when the experiment was repeated the result was the same. A magnetic needle and a compass also followed Kluski's hand movements. A few days later, a séance was held by a circle of friends in Kluski's presence. Dr Sokołowski, without warning the medium (by then definitely identified as Kluski) or explaining anything to anyone, placed a container with liquid paraffin wax on the table and a paraffin mould the size of a man's hand was found after the séance.

Kluski's recorded mediumship lasted from 1918 to 1925. There were about 340 sittings, the great majority of which took place at Kluski's own apartment. Of that total, about 50 were at friends' houses, and 34 took place abroad. Fourteen of those which took place abroad, from

November 1920 to January 1921, are significant because they were conducted under laboratory conditions and their evidence sets the standard against which the less formal events need to be measured. There was a definite development of mediumship, from the less sophisticated phenomena such as knocks and movements of objects, to self-illuminating, life-like interactive apparitions. These séances are the ones recorded by Okołowicz and published in book form. However, there are also other sources for Kluski sittings, and I have tried to include these wherever possible.

The séances reported by Okołowicz divide into three periods. The first phase, from December 1918 to November 1920, was the beginning of Kluski's mediumship. Both the medium and the sitters were unprepared for and overwhelmed by the number and variety of phenomena which were taking place spontaneously and simultaneously. To give an example, a séance held during the second half of 1919 resulted in a pyramid of objects which would be impossible to arrange by normal means. When the light was turned on, the table was in the middle of the circle, on it was a chair with three legs on the table and one leg in the air. To keep it balanced a heavy wooden column, 140 cm high, was placed on it, and on top a heavy bronze candlestick was balancing the column. The pyramid almost reached the ceiling and, on seeing it, the participants rushed to support it because they thought it would fall down on them.

At that stage, the medium was also very actively interested in the phenomena. There was thus an abundance of ideas as to how to investigate them and a variety of attempts to implement these ideas. This meant that systematic observation and chronological recording were difficult to achieve, resulting in somewhat fragmentary documentation which was limited to the most important facts. There are about a dozen reports from that period, mainly describing séances which included the taking of photographs.

It was only during the second half of 1919 that both the medium and the sitters began to impose a framework on the proceedings which would allow more detailed observation of the phenomena themselves and the possibility of investigating the conditions which influenced their appearance and development. Attempts to impose a pre-planned programme on séances meant that they began to lose their improvised character.

At the end of 1919 and the beginning of 1920 there were relatively fewer materialising séances, and more automatic writing séances which were less exhausting for the medium. However, the dominance of automatic writing seemed to have a negative effect on the richness of the materialising séances, which then became of poorer quality.

In 1920, after the Bolshevik attack on Poland, Kluski served in the army as a volunteer, and séances were suspended until the autumn of that year. They then continued, with stronger materialising phenomena, until Kluski's departure for Paris.

The second period, apart from a few séances in Warsaw, mainly covers the evidence gathered by the French researchers at IMI in Paris, from November 1920 until February 1921, and Kluski's other séances abroad. Geley's reports have been accused of too much summarising instead of giving blow-by-blow accounts; nevertheless, they include plenty of detail, particularly on the subject of controls. Also, whilst being very lucid and readable, they correspond closely to reports from other séances by other witnesses, which must go at least some way towards confirming their credibility and authenticity.

During that period Kluski's health deteriorated seriously. He began to be increasingly exhausted by the sittings, as well as becoming more passive during them, showing a tendency to fall into prolonged trance. He began to leave the initiative to the participants and after a séance would remember almost nothing of the events. On the one hand, this condition of the medium made conducting séances more difficult since extra care was needed to protect his health. On the other, it made it much easier to observe the phenomena. According to Okołowicz, the Paris sittings played a significant part in the deterioration of Kluski's health. Kluski was not given to discussing his psychological states and, in the interest of science, submitted to the various, sometimes very oppressive, forms of control and new initiatives stoically and patiently. However, on leaving Paris his physical and psychological condition was very poor, and for approximately six months after returning home his health did not return to normal.

It would not have helped that the pressure to hold séances did not diminish after Kluski left France. A number of séances took place in Italy and Austria, as Kluski travelled to these countries to stay with friends who turned out to be keen to experience the phenomena. Séances were held in Florence and Vienna, and while the conditions under which they took place can fairly be described as chaotic, their very spontaneity, together with the randomness of the witnesses who were totally new to Kluski as a medium, could be argued to provide further confirmation of the séances being genuine. Okołowicz quotes a report (sent to him) of a séance in Florence on 21 January 1921, in the dining room of the

"Select" boarding house, via dei Fossi 16, in the presence of 16 persons, where five phantoms appeared almost simultaneously, whilst various objects, including a heavy oak table weighing more than 150 kg, were lifted in the air. The séance was interrupted by participants who were overcome by the phenomena, and the medium fell to the floor and could not be awoken from a heavy trance. At a séance on 27 January 1921 in Vienna, organised by some acquaintances of Kluski, partially materialised figures could be observed in the light from the street lamps, as well as lighting themselves with their own light and the screens (usually these were wooden boards like large hand mirrors, covered with a luminous substance). Unsystematic and fragmentary though they are, the witnesses' statements describe the kinds of phenomena which correspond closely to those experienced under controlled conditions.

The third period lasted between February 1921 and the end of March 1925, and included the richest phenomena representing the most developed phase of Kluski's mediumship. The early séances during that period demanded a great deal of effort from the medium, whose health continued to deteriorate. Exhausted, sick and apathetic, the medium would fall into a deep, yet troubled, trance immediately at the beginning of the séance, and would stay in that state for nearly 9/10 of the duration. He would regain consciousness with difficulty and, in contrast to the initial period of mediumship, would be unable to carry on with another sitting (early séances might include as many as three half-hour or so sittings interrupted by short breaks). These later séances would last longer, sometimes for more than an hour. During the first half of 1921 the number of séances was not large, but they were held under very strict controls, with the medium totally passive. During that period the number of isolated phenomena and movements began to diminish, giving way to better materialisations of human apparitions. The séances became much quieter and more systematic. In addition, almost all violent phenomena such as loud noises and the crashing of furniture, as well as those taking place at a distance from the medium, resulted in Kluski becoming short of breath and convulsing. This would last for as long as the phenomenon manifested itself, even though there was no interruption in the trance state. These reactions did not appear to have any obvious link to the phenomena, yet gave the impression of his organism being violently forced to produce emanations of some kind. This state of affairs lasted for more than a year and then began to recede. Later the convulsions and breathlessness became less frequent, and only the vomiting remained frequent.

At the beginning of that period, something like a "fluid" or an energy seemed to emanate from the medium on frequent occasions, like a stream about 1 metre wide, at the height of a human being, flowing violently around the room. It seemed able to move small objects in an undirected manner. It could be compared to a fast moving magnet, but it affected all sorts of things, not just metal but wood, papers, books, etc. Sometimes it would branch in various directions while the medium would shake. It was usually preceded by small lights giving out a heavy yellow phosphorescent vapour.

Towards the end of 1921 there was a significant decrease in the quantity of the small lights and the emergence of increasingly powerful nebulae, strongly phosphorescent and emitting a very refreshing smell of ozone. Also during that period there appeared phantoms which are difficult to describe, since there seemed to be two or even three figures filling the same shape simultaneously. It was clearly established in the light of the screen that, observed continuously, the face of the figure would become clearly male without losing some of the features and accessories of a woman, and the reverse. This seemed to depend on the dominant impression experienced by the participants at a given time. During the séances there were again noises (throughout the room), but not so clearly associated with the simultaneous convulsions of the medium. These sounds sometimes gave the impression of children, or small animals, which every now and again would become out of control and start noisily frolicking in the dark in the corners of the room.

The first months of 1922 passed quietly for the medium. There were no séances except for those involving automatic writing, which usually took place in the presence of one or two persons and were of a personal character. During that period there was also some improvement in Kluski's health, both physically and mentally. From the end of March of that year there were more appearances of phantoms in human form recognised by participants as deceased relatives. During the last three months of 1922, Okołowicz discerned further improvement in the medium's condition. Kluski became less apathetic and more frequently showed interest in life outside of the séances. As for the séances themselves, by then they seemed to be of no interest to Kluski. He became increasingly passive, falling into a deep trance which on many occasions lasted continuously throughout the séance. The trance would usually come within a few minutes of the light being extinguished. Awakening would be slow, but usually calm. It would take place when the chain of hands was broken or when the controls were stopped. Only when the medium started the séance in an agitated and nervous state would the trance be uneven and agitated too. On such occasions the awakening would also be difficult, either quick with groans and vomiting, or very slow and heavy-going.

The course of the séances, as well as the phenomena, began to be characterised by greater freedom and ease. The phenomena seem to be created according to a deliberate design. In all the aspects of mediumship there was less heaviness and less impression of being forced, although a state of weakness and confusion continued to overcome the medium after the séances and would last a long time. Slowly, there seemed to emerge an apparent link with phenomena from previous years, with the appearance of the same or similar phantoms and isolated phenomena, which seemed like a continuation of, or a supplement to, the previous ones. The phenomena did not have the same force and vigour as those from the first half of 1919, but they were more cheerful and kept improving in terms of clarity.

At that time phantoms of military figures, mostly Polish, appeared with increasing frequency. These apparitions were very varied in their looks, age and rank, and were very often recognised as friends or relatives of those present. However, among these military figures there were also those which did not seem to resemble any familiar deceased persons. Such apparitions would then be visible for a short time and did not seem to try to enter into any special contact with those present.

At the end of May 1923, Kluski's mediumship took on a new character. Human figures and lights became dominant and other phenomena became less fragmentary, transforming gradually into observable activities carried out by fully materialised apparitions which showed themselves in increasingly perfect form and increasingly beautiful light. Almost every phenomenon appeared simultaneously with the apparition, frequently allowing the observers to determine which phenomenon should be ascribed to which apparition. New, extraordinarily rich and strong light phenomena, with clear shapes and colours, began to dominate over the familiar lights regarded as typical of Kluski. There were increasing numbers of self-illuminating apparitions and the phantoms were more frequently of a Christian nature, with symbols such as a luminous cross introducing an elevated, spiritual atmosphere.

At the same time, a significant difference began to be apparent between phantoms showing themselves in the light of a screen, and those which illuminated themselves with their own light. The latter were less numerous but incomparably more perfect in their appearance.

While about half of the phantoms which illuminated themselves with a screen were recognised as those of deceased persons known to the participants during their lifetime, those emitting their own strong light were of a different nature. The dignified appearance of some of them sometimes resembled famous historical figures or types characteristic of ancient epochs, both Eastern and European.

Okołowicz provides some rough figures: thus, during the first period (November 1918 – November/December 1920), the average length of a séance would be about 30 minutes, but there might be two or three sittings held on the same evening, interspersed with suitable breaks. Kluski would remain conscious for about a third of the time. During the second period (November 1920 – February 1921) the séances lengthened, up to about 45 minutes, and the amount of time that the medium remained conscious diminished by about half. In the third period (March 1921 – March 1925) séances lasted about 60 minutes on average, and the medium would be in full trance for more than 90% of that time. These approximations do not apply to the séances when attempts were made to take photographs and the medium would try to stay awake.

Although the year 1925 was not the end of Kluski's mediumship, the emphasis seemed to have shifted from physical phenomena to automatic writing, the surviving information on which is very scant. However, we do know that Kluski still had the power to produce physical phenomena, since they were witnessed in 1928 by Dr Eugene Osty, Director of IMI in Paris. Osty came to Warsaw to conduct séances with other mediums, but he also visited Kluski and reported this in a letter quoted in the journal the Polish SPR: "The séance with M. Kluski [...] was extremely interesting. It was short, because M. Kluski suffered an attack of nausea, but for me it was sufficient. I witnessed, in the bright light of a luminous screen, the quick formation of two paraffin gloves. This is truly extraordinary! One can only be extremely sorry that M.Kluski does not devote his life to mediumship, which finds such powerful expression in him."[1]

---

[1] Quoted by Dr F. Habdank to whom the letter was addressed, in *Zagadnienia Metapsychiczne* 19-20, 1928, 85.

3.2. Conditions and controls

Geley's laboratory experiments

The only séances with Kluski held in a laboratory were the ones which took place at the International Metapsychic Institute in Paris in 1920. In his *Clairvoyance and Materialization*, Geley describes the conditions under which they took place, in the section *How the sittings were conducted* (Geley 1927: 207-212). They provide a useful starting point of reference for the kind and extent of controls employed at the other séances.

There were eleven successful sittings and three with either no results or insignificant ones. With one exception they all took place at the IMI laboratory, a room with no windows and with two entrance doors which were always locked after the entrance of the medium and the experimenters. For lighting they used a red 50 candle[2] power lamp the position of which, and the intensity of light, could be adjusted, as well as large screens coated with sulphide of zinc and provided with a handle, which were used intermittently. The light used during the experiments was sufficient to show the outlines of the medium and the experimenters.

The medium sat in an ordinary chair in front of the dark cabinet, which was not used. The controls consisted, essentially, of the medium's hands being held by the experimenters on his right and left. The experimenters also pressed against the medium's legs and knees, so that he could not make a move without it being felt. Kluski remained almost perfectly still throughout the séances, only placing his head on the table in front of him or on the shoulder of one of the controllers once he was entranced. His hands would not move at all. Geley emphasises the fact that they were all well aware of the trick of hand substitution, which was never attempted by Kluski. In Geley's words: "In the experiment of November 15 [1920] (one of the most striking) Professor Richet held the left hand, and I held the right. During the trance I gently moved the hand I held towards that held by Richet, so that I could feel the two hands of the medium and that of Professor Richet all at the same time. During this period we had luminous phenomena, touches, and the production of a mould of a materialised hand." (pp.

---

[2] One candle (candela) is approximately the amount of light produced by a single candle.

210-11) Additionally, the experimenters would from time to time confirm aloud which hand they were holding, and made a special effort to observe the immobility of the medium.

Kluski was not undressed nor searched, but was subjected to medical examination by Geley both before and after the experiments, who was thus able to check discreetly that nothing suspicious was present.

During the experiments, the researchers (who, apart from Geley, included Charles Richet, Count de Gramont, Count Julian Potocki, Camille Flammarion and his wife) would take their seats, link hands, and the controllers would make sure in full light that they were holding the right and left hand of the medium. The red light would be dimmed and they would converse until the phenomena began, which at successful séances was almost immediately. The séance would last for about half an hour followed by a break for a rest, following the same pattern as Kluski's early séances in Warsaw.

At the time of Geley's experiments, Kluski entered the state of semi-trance easily and at will, staying conscious during the séance to observe the phenomena (but not to try and will them, which had a negative effect). Sometimes, however, this would deepen into complete unconsciousness, when the phenomena would become more pronounced. His exhaustion after the experiments was extreme, to the point of fainting, with perspiration, great thirst and occasional palpitations of the heart.

Geley divides what was observed into categories of phenomena, instead of providing accounts of consecutive events (Okołowicz provides both). He makes a case against the very possibility of fraud on the basis of not only the location (laboratory) and the controls maintained during the séances, but on the basis of what was observed during the séances and whether it could be produced fraudulently. He emphasises that the possibility of fraud is discussed for the sake of the readers, while the experimenters have not the slightest doubt as to the veracity of the phenomena.

Starting with the light phenomena, which he regards as the "primary substance" produced by Kluski prior to materialisations, he discusses the possibility of producing them fraudulently.

According to him, the only means of imitating little lights and creating them artificially is the use of phosphorescent substance. However, the lights produced at the Kluski sittings had different shapes, dimensions, and consistencies. They also appeared and disappeared very suddenly, as well as suddenly or gradually increasing or decreasing in size.

The lights were numerous and scattered, flying far from the medium. They could not have been caused by flares thrown up and then falling down, or produced by the use of substances such as ferro-cerrum, on the contrary, they were purposeful, and often associated with the touches and materialisations. Any attempt to explain this by postulating human hands with fingers dipped in a phosphorescent substance would have to ignore the fact that the phenomena were taking place in a laboratory under experimental conditions. In Geley's words:

"The distance of the lights, the multiplicity of the phenomena, the variations of luminosity, the forms and faces, could never have been imitated by a single liberated hand." (Geley 1927:217)

Geley deals in a similar way with the issue of materialised faces, which were observed at all the séances at IMI. In the locked laboratory, with the medium immobilised on both sides and with the red light turned on, they saw apparitions with human faces of natural size, which usually appeared above the heads of the medium and those present, and which illuminated themselves with the screen. The experimenters could see faces but not the whole body and on some occasions materialised busts.

Geley dismisses the supposition of collective hallucinations (it would have to be collective, since everyone reported the same impressions), and concentrates on the hypothesis of fraud. To achieve the phenomena fraudulently would require the help of one or more accomplices, or the possibility of the medium changing and moving his face, or the use of masks worn on the hand. None of these would have been possible under the séance conditions. Unauthorised entry would have been impossible, the medium was held at all times, and his head often rested on Geley's shoulder whilst living, intelligent faces were materialising above the participants at the same time. The same applies to the possibility of the medium operating masks.[3]

Moreover, the phantoms seen by Geley and other experimenters on later occasions and in other locations (such as the séance on 25 December 1921 at the residence of Jules Roche) were familiar not only to them from earlier séances (e.g., an old woman with her head covered with a grey kerchief), but sound familiar from the descriptions of other participants in other circumstances. Clearly, any explanation involving the use of masks and/or accomplices also implies their availability at all

---

[3] In his *Clairvoyance and Materialization* Geley devotes a section to "Pseudo-materialisations and pseudo-mediums", demonstrating a thorough knowledge of possible tricks (Geley 1927:390-95).

times, including spontaneous impromptu events with a random selection of witnesses. Another feature which speaks against the employment of confederates or props is the fact that the apparitions were not always perfect, a point made by F. W. Pawłowski[4] when describing the séances led by Okołowicz which he attended in Warsaw. Sometimes they were partial or undersized, "two thirds even one-half of the natural size. When I first saw such an apparition, I thought it was that of a child, but a closer examination revealed the wrinkled face of an old man or woman, only undersized. The leader of the séance would say then 'Let us help the medium' (a technical term in this circle), and would begin to beat time, so that the sitters might breathe simultaneously and deeply. The effect of this procedure is wonderful: the undersized apparition grows and in several seconds reaches full size." (Pawłowski 1925: 502)

Reports by Okołowicz

In his archives, Okołowicz had more than 200 séances recorded by himself, and 150 recorded by others. No reports were made of those séances at which people sat randomly as they wished, since that meant that the controls were poor and the phenomena chaotic. It was a learning process about how to achieve the best conditions, and the influence of participants on the quality of mediumship. As the routines developed, it became possible to keep very detailed records. Simultaneous note-taking would clearly not have been possible during the séances but apart from his own notes, over a period of several days, Okołowicz would also collect accounts from the other participants, particularly the non-regular ones, first-timers and the more nervous ones. All the reports of "official" séances list the names of the sitters who also signed the joint reports.

Conditions

The majority of the séances with Kluski took place in Warsaw in his apartment located on the top floor of a four-storey block in the centre of

---

[4] F.W. Pawłowski, Professor of Aeronautical Engineering at the University of Michigan, published his account of Kluski sittings in the *Journal of the American Society for Psychical Research* in September 1925. His nephew, a high-ranking official at the Polish Ministry of Foreign Affairs, was a close friend of the Modrzejewski family.

Warsaw. It was a large apartment (136 m^2) with high ceilings (4m)[5], the location and size not unusual for someone of his professional standing. The séances were held in Kluski's study, described in consistent terms in a number of reports by different participants. Okołowicz provides drawings which show the position of furniture and the grouping of participants. For what he terms "official" (properly recorded) séances, the room would be searched prior to the séance and the door to the study would stay locked throughout with the key remaining in the lock.

Figure 2: *Typical seating arrangement. A – phosphorescent screen;*
B – furniture; M – medium; numbers indicate participants; drzwi – door;
okno – window; piec – stove. A red lamp would usually be placed on the stove.

Clearly, it is impossible to rule out collusion on the grounds of such information alone. However, we also need to bear in mind that over a quarter of Kluski's séances (more than 90) took place in other locations, mostly in friends' apartments in Warsaw, and a further 34 took place abroad, including those conducted in Geley's laboratory at the IMI. A number of them took place in Italy in hotel rooms and at the Polish Consulate, away from Kluski's usual sitters. In all the reports of these sittings the phenomena described are similar, and similarly impossible to produce fraudulently without an elaborate setup involving accomplices.

In a typical séance in Kluski's study there would be a weak red light, which would usually be expected to turn itself off, and the only source of illumination would be the phosphorescent screens. The light from these depended on the quality of the luminous paint. At first it would be bright enough to read by but would weaken after about 20 minutes. However, the light phenomena (including the later self-illuminating

<hr>

[5] Information obtained from Warsaw archive office.

apparitions) could be very bright and sometimes lit the whole room. Sometimes there would be other sources of light as well, such as full size screens, blinds not drawn, and clocks with luminous digits.

According to Geley, the use of screens was an inconvenience, since they only lit the apparition for one person and only within the limits of their light. Although cheating was not possible in the IMI séances (at least, not without the knowledge of the experimenters), under other circumstances the use of screens could make it easier to cheat. In his book, Okołowicz takes issue with this view, on the basis of nearly six years of experiments. Only a small percentage of materialisations in Kluski's séances illuminated themselves with their own light, while the rest appeared against, or in the reflection of, the light emanating from the screen. Without the use of screens a large number of apparitions, figures, and faces could not have been observed. The calm light of the screens was also less disturbing to the medium and, at the same time, could be compared by the observers to the light created by the apparitions, and enabled them to note the development and intensity of the latter.

During the later séances, the medium would usually quickly fall into a trance and stay unconscious, but in the early stages of mediumship he would often remain conscious, or semi-conscious. Furthermore, he would also try to stay conscious with the help of the controllers, when photographs were attempted, in order to avoid the shock of the magnesium flashlight. In fact, this usually meant that on those occasions the phenomena were poorer, while his exhaustion and haemorrhaging after the séance would be more intense. Altogether, 15 photographs had been taken, 13 of them successfully. They relate to the earlier séances, when the phenomena tended to be more turbulent and kinetic, and less luminous.

There were no regular arrangements for measuring temperature during the séances. It would normally rise during the sitting, and for this reason the participants usually aimed for about 18° C to start with, but sometimes the temperature would suddenly fall, once in September 1920 by 10° C towards the end of the sitting. It returned to normal immediately after the séance, but the medium's body was very hot as usual.

Controlling the medium

The Polish investigators were well aware of the various methods of controlling a medium and, according to Okołowicz, in the early stages of Kluski's mediumship the most elaborate controls were employed, and often repeated in different variants as new researchers flowed in. These controls were applied both in his apartment and in those of his friends. They had the medium tied up and put in a net and used seals, but this did not stop the phenomena, only acting as an irritant by forcing Kluski to adopt unnatural positions. Once it was established that regardless of the controls the phenomena were the same, the more intrusive methods were avoided so as not to exhaust and hurt the medium. Kluski did, in fact, sit totally naked for Geley and Richet in Warsaw in 1922 (24 April), but this did not stop the phenomena from appearing. Eventually, the researchers settled on controllers on either side of the medium holding his hands and touching his legs with theirs.

The usual number of participants would be 6 to 8 people, as greater numbers were tiring for the medium. In about 75% of the séances, a closed circle would be formed, and when photographs were attempted, they would form a semicircle. The duration of a usual séance was between 30 minutes to an hour. The best atmosphere was created by easy-going and relaxed conversation. Regular participants were often assigned tasks. One would observe the order of the phenomena, another their timing, and yet another their appearance and formation. Someone would be assigned to watching out for the results of spoken interventions by participants, someone else might watch the condition of the medium, etc.

3.3. The medium and the sitters

Kluski seemed to exert a degree of conscious influence on the séances. Sometimes he would issue what might be described as instructions to himself before the séance, such as (on 23 March 1924) that no apparition should be similar to him, or (on 28 July 1923), that he should not tremble. His constant wish was that no participant should be hurt, and all of these seemed to be influenced by his will. There is also an interesting account of a séance held at an apartment of Kluski's friends in February 1921 when it was decided, against Kluski's wishes, that a séance should be held, he (as he later told Okołowicz) was determined not to let the phenomena develop. After the light was turned out, Okołowicz clearly saw little lights, nebulae and what looked like folds of white material creeping around Kluski's head and upper chest which did not move away from him despite the urgent requests of the participants. This carried on while Kluski was awake and talking, but suddenly Okołowicz heard a deep sigh, which usually preceded the medium falling into trance, and the lights and nebulae flew away from him. A similar sequence of events could be observed at the séances for which photographs were planned and, when the medium tried to stay awake to avoid the shock of the flashlight, he would suddenly fall asleep and the phenomena would suddenly intensify.

By the time Kluski was ready to sit down for a séance, he would almost invariably have spent the day busy with his professional duties. This would affect his mood and condition in the evening and also seemed to affect the phenomena. When he was exhausted, the phenomena would be apathetic and form slowly and, when he was alert and cheerful, the phenomena seemed to form without effort. If he drank alcohol prior to a séance, the phenomena were likely to be fast, noisy, kinetic, and chaotic, with apparitions looking more like the medium.

At the time of entering the trance state, Kluski seemed to be particularly sensitive to those around him. He was observed to read their thoughts and be aware of their physical condition, to the point of being able to tell them what they had eaten a few hours prior to the séance.

Particularly during the later period of Kluski's mediumship, the participants tended to forget the presence of the medium as the phenomena developed because he seemed absent. All of his life force seemed to have been directed to the phantoms and his presence was only remembered when he started to tremble or when one of the phantoms illuminated him and, on such occasions, he appeared as if dead. A participant compared this (October 1920) to a cannon being melted down; for a while it retains its external shape even though it is empty inside, since all the metal has flowed out from the inside and has become part of the other molten metals. It seemed to the participants that the more alive the apparitions seemed, the more like a husk was the appearance of the medium.

During the final period of his mediumship, Kluski also remained virtually unconscious for much longer following a séance, for about half an hour. This was not like the trance state but more like a state of confusion and weakness, as if after enormous exertion. Efforts to revive him were fruitless. He would appear semi-conscious, with eyes unfocused, unable to stand unaided, and unable to answer questions. The return to consciousness would be sudden, with the whole body shaken, eyes regaining intelligent expression and an immediate return to normal behaviour. One of the doctors who attended a séance commented that you just could not fake the physical appearance presented by Kluski afterwards. After a séance there would also be a blunting of his senses; he could not distinguish water from tea or alcohol when given a drink, and would have difficulty recognising individual people, except generally being able to tell the séance participants from the others. After a séance which was suddenly interrupted, instead of being gradually brought to a controlled conclusion, things would be even worse, sometimes causing a swelling of his face and making the smell of ozone emanate from his whole body for some days. Sometimes on the morning after a séance his body would be covered in large, sometimes bleeding and suppurative wounds which would disappear without a trace after two days at the most, without ever leaving a scar (séance 24 April 1922). On one occasion, when Kluski forgot to empty his pockets as he usually did prior to a séance, after the séance a red painful area, as if of a burn, shaped exactly like a fob watch with a chain, was found on his body in the place where the watch had been.

He would be very hungry and eat enormous quantities once the confusion and exhaustion had passed, but the most striking feature was his great thirst after the séance and the fact that, during the séance, he would perspire profusely even though he did not under normal circumstances. Towards the end of the third period he increasingly suffered digestive problems and bouts of violent and persistent nausea during and towards the end of séances. This would cause him to cease sittings for quite long intervals.

41

There also seemed to be quite a close relationship and a constant interplay between the mental and emotional states of the medium, the phenomena, and the participants. Not much attention was paid to this aspect during the first phase of Kluski's mediumship, when even the medium himself was involved in investigating the phenomena, but more systematic observations were made in the later periods. Okołowicz describes in some detail the procedures developed to obtain the best results, as well as the kinds of sitters who would be most effective.

Thus, during a séance, the main roles were those of the controllers and the leader (most often Okołowicz himself). The controllers, apart from keeping watch, would try to keep the medium calm and passive. The leader's task would be to maintain the right mood and to direct the proceedings. Best results were obtained when both the controllers and leader were experienced and well known to the medium. It was also important that the controllers should be in robust health, both physically and mentally, since their state would affect Kluski's state after the sitting. Sometimes the participants could perceptibly influence the medium's state. In one report the medium started out irritated and gloomy but became cheerful by the end of the séance after a concerted effort was made by the participants.

Deep breathing by all the sitters helped when the medium groaned or trembled, usually when noisy kinetic phenomena were taking place. It seemed as if the regular movement was being transferred to the medium and calming him, as it did the participants. The trembling was most intense in 1921 and 1922, later less so. The trembling seemed to happen when the medium's body was emanating something which as yet did not have any form, and became less violent when the phenomena reached their climax. A similar movement transfer was also employed successfully when, for example, before the end of the séance the medium would lean his head against the edge of the table and seemed not to react to the breathing. Everyone would then put their heads down on the edge of the table and then lift them, with the result that the medium, without waking, would imitate the movement and breathe more easily by straightening up.

The end of a séance seemed to come about naturally, by a kind of inner agreement by everyone that this should happen, and in most cases the medium would wake up normally with the help of the participants (this might involve saying his name, the hand-chain being broken, and the light coming on, all happening in a calm and gradual manner). This was particularly important during the third phase of Kluski's mediumship when the trance state was very deep. If anyone wanted to continue or became too involved in a particular phenomenon to let go, the waking up process would be difficult.

When it was agreed that the séance was to end, there was usually a period of passive waiting, which became more lively when the red light came on (usually by itself) and the medium emerged into a semi-trance. If the lamp did not turn itself on, kinetic phenomena would often resume (such as things being thrown on the floor), distracting the participants from the medium who would then wake up with a sigh and ask for water. Interruption of the trance state did not always entail the end of phenomena, and the reverse also happened: the phenomena might stop suddenly even when the medium was still deep in trance. On three occasions the phenomena stopped when one of the participants tried to imitate them by knocking, touching others, etc.

Of the 350 or so people who took part in the sittings with Kluski, most had a positive influence, and age, gender or profession did not seem to make much difference. Negative influence came mainly from sceptics and uncritical believers, but Okołowicz claims that everyone who attended more than once became totally convinced of the reality of the phenomena. However, regardless of their opinions and beliefs, all those attending the séances treated the apparitions as if they were real individuals.

The kind of person who made a positive contribution to a sitting would be someone mature, cheerful, balanced, and in good shape physically and mentally. People with weak health and of neurotic dispositions, even when this was a temporary state, would be likely to have a negative effect. In the later phase of Kluski's mediumship, when people prepared for séances by eating no meat and not drinking alcohol, the phenomena tended to be particularly rich and serious, with the predominance of exotic phantoms, and the medium did not subsequently suffer the usual painful physical complaints.

The participants influenced the phenomena indirectly by telling the medium about their expectations and their wishes before the séance, as well as during the séance, by commenting on the phenomena prior to the medium reaching trance state. Once the medium was in a trance, the participants seemed to have a degree of direct influence on the observable events. (See pp 110-115 for Okołowicz's attempt to correlate the participants' thoughts and the events at a séance aimed at producing paraffin moulds). However, a sudden change in the desired outcome would have a negative influence on the events. Okołowicz quotes such an example from a séance in April 1919 at the apartment of Kluski's friend (in Warsaw). There were two vases on top of the wardrobe in the room and the participants asked for one of them to be brought to the table. Everyone supported this wish and, in the light coming from the insufficiently covered window, the vase could be seen rising in the air and noiselessly moving above the heads of the participants to land in the middle of the table. Some participants then asked for the second vase to be moved in this way and it began to happen. However, one of the participants called out, "Please touch me," when the vase was close to him. He was then touched on his head and shoulder, but at the same time the vase fell to the floor and shattered.

Okołowicz's conclusion is thus that the best attitude was to be alert but calm and on the whole passive, trying to support the medium rather than to affect the phenomena, while the worst was to try and impose one's will on them or try to draw them to oneself, which would make them weaken and disappear. Since Kluski was very much his own person, this may have involved his reaction to attempts at bullying.

The best sitters adapted easily and seemed to know intuitively how to behave. Sometimes they would be given a "mark of distinction" by having their backs rubbed, as if the apparitions drew strength from them. They would also display, to a degree, some of the reactions of the medium, such as pain on being suddenly exposed to light, and a state of exhaustion and confusion after the séance. In one report, there seems to be a link between the appearance of a phantom of a Japanese girl, and one of the female sitters complaining of "pulling" around her eyes and mouth (pp 55). In another (13 March 1924), a participant with the left hand in a sling after suffering inflammation seems to influence the appearance of the phantoms which have a problem using their left hands, while the medium's left hand becomes painful as well.

Interestingly, the assorted family pets, cats and dogs, were on the whole uniformly adamant in their refusal to be involved in the séances (from displays of anxiety to terror) and avoided the medium at such times, however fond of their master under normal circumstances. On the other hand, the family cat's behaviour after the séances could be quite remarkable: it would either refuse to enter, or rush in and search, behaving more like a dog. If there was a residue in the form of ozone stains or phosphorescent spots after a séance, it would either smell them carefully or would rub itself against them in what appeared to be ecstasy.

3.4. The phenomena

Classifying the range of Kluski phenomena reveals that they fall into categories which are well established in physical mediumship, even though some aspects of their manifestations might be on a more spectacular scale. This is reassuring to know, since at a later stage we can examine them in the context of accounts about other mediums.

Sounds

Knockings, as if with the fingers or hand, close to the medium, on the table, walls, chairs and furniture close by, also took place outside the séances, in full light, and happened almost on a daily basis. Sounds of rustling, rubbing, rapping, animal noises, and occasional whispers (sometimes outside séances) featured in most descriptions. In 1919 and 1920 there were occasions when sounds were heard as if of grain scattering, but no grain was found on the premises.

Human voices were usually in whispers. Speaking voices at the séances were hardly ever loud enough to be heard by everyone present (Kluski's voice was very weak). Singing or whistling were the more frequent phenomena, and more voices featured at the sittings towards the end of the final period of Kluski's mediumship. However, when close by, the apparitions seemed to have breath, heartbeat, and even tummy rumblings. There were also groans and sighs, and of course communication by "knocking" the alphabet.

Kinetic phenomena

As has already been stated, during the early séances (1919), the kinetic phenomena would be violent and chaotic, with furniture piled up in ways impossible to achieve by normal means, and objects hurtling about in a frightening fashion. However, even during that period, the kinetic phenomena seemed to be associated with the presence of a human phantom, although Okołowicz does not explain why this was thought to be the case. The change in the phenomena, from movement of objects towards apparitions, may have been related to the preferences of the medium and the participants for the appearance of phantoms, and of lights, since the predominance of kinetic phenomena meant that there were fewer lights.

The turning on and off of lights might also be counted among the kinetic phenomena, although most of the time it seemed like momentary isolation in the electric circuit, and not the turning on and off of the switch (which remained turned on) or unplugging the lamp.

Among the kinetic phenomena one might also include breezes and touches, of which there was a great variety, from the lightest, as if by a child, to firm handshakes and thumps on the back, which in some form featured in every séance.

Apports

Apports were quite frequent in the early séances, mainly of things from other rooms in the apartment: flowers, hats, an apple on a branch with a leaf which disappeared after being examined (17 March 1920), and once a soda syphon. On 16 July 1919 three of the participants marked in secret a cigar in a newly opened box of 50 and placed it in the bottom of the box. The box was closed and placed on a table under the light in a room three rooms away from Kluski's study where the séance was held. During the séance one of the participants said, "Please bring the object only we know about," and a few seconds later a cigar was put in the hand of a participant sitting 2 metres from the medium. After the séance ended it was found to be the marked cigar and the box was in the same position in the same room as previously. Other objects were sometimes also brought from outside, but these phenomena ceased in the later years.

Under this heading one might include the only occasion when the medium disappeared from the séance room during a séance. During a very successful sitting in August 1919 it was noticed that the phenomena were weakening. At that time, the medium was sitting on a chair in the middle of the room, and the participants formed a hand-chain around him. As the phenomena stopped it was found that the medium's chair was empty and, on turning on the light, he was found to be absent from the room. The participants, worried, started searching and found him in another room in the apartment, fast asleep on a settee. On being woken up he had no recollection of what happened and the last thing he remembered was falling into trance. Before the participants left the séance room they had established that the door to the séance room was undoubtedly locked and the key was in the lock on the inside.

Change of weight

This may have happened more frequently than has been recorded, since no attempts were usually made to weigh the medium as the participants would concentrate on the production of more exciting phenomena. However, Okołowicz describes a situation after one of the séances, when he returned to the study and found Kluski lying motionless on the settee. He realised that the medium had not woken up from his trance, which was a cataleptic one and manifested itself by the total rigidity of the body and spasmodically curled fingers. Usually in such cases Okołowicz would try to open Kluski's fist by force, thus inducing the usual semi-trance state, from which Kluski could emerge by himself. Wanting to do this carefully so as not to damage the medium's hand muscles, Okołowicz decided to place him in a more comfortable position and noticed with surprise that he was extremely light. To make sure, he pressed very lightly on Kluski's legs which stuck out almost to the knees from the settee. This was sufficient for the whole body to spring into a vertical position. Having tried this a number of times with similar results, Okołowicz put his hand under Kluski's hips and tried to lift him. This was easily achieved and he had the impression that the medium had lost at least two thirds of his normal weight (ca 66 kg). When finally, after a lot of effort, Okołowicz managed to unclench the fist, the whole body, stiff until then, regained its normal state of flexibility, and when he immediately afterwards tried to lift Kluski he found that his weight was back to normal. A few moments later Kluski revived and in a sleepy voice complained about the heat, also asking for water, which was an indication that he was recovering in the usual way.

Lights

On 25 March 1923 Okołowicz presented a paper on the subject of Kluski's "light phenomena" to the Polish SPR, which he also included in his book and which I summarise here. This is a much more detailed and varied analysis than the descriptions of the Kluski lights provided by Geley (Geley 1927: 213-217), but in the main it concerns the same phenomena. Geley interpreted them as the exteriorisation of what he called the "primary substance", and the first stage of the materialisation phenomena.

Although the light phenomena were not unconnected and merged into each other, the following main groups could be distinguished:

1. Round, greenish, slow-moving lights, about 1 cm in diameter and not emitting any smell. Such lights also appeared in Kluski's mouth outside the séances.

2. Triangular or elliptical larger greenish lights. They appeared first as a nebula with a brighter middle, which would then open up with a sound like lips "popping", to show a shrinking centre. They were short-lived and much faster and more energetic than the lights described in 1.

Both kinds of lights moved through the medium, the participants and the surrounding objects (usually with a knocking sound). Those through whom the lights travelled felt them go in and come out. Both groups of lights could appear far from the medium.

3. Lights which tended to appear in the middle or at the end of the séance. They were highly phosphorescent and smelled of ozone (identified as such by the chemists present, such as Dr Nencki). They gave the impression of being attached to human extremities and faces. Their movements resembled human movements and most often they appeared close to the medium. Sometimes they made a knocking, clapping, or rubbing sound, and they might be compared to little fires which cluster and separate. Yellow-greenish in colour, sometimes so much vapour emanated from them that they formed nebulae. They left the medium confused, even though they did not affect his mood as badly as did the kinetic phenomena. Okołowicz also counted among these the light spots which appeared on the medium's body. They appeared all over the body and were mobile, like a luminous liquid, moving slowly and smelling of ozone and, on being touched, gave the impression that the movement took place under the skin (although sometimes after touching such a spot one had on one's hand a trace of a fatty liquid smelling of ozone). Sometimes they disappeared as if they were falling deep into the body, only to reappear at another point. If they were more shimmery they exuded phosphorescent vapours which also smelled of ozone. The size of such a luminous spot was no bigger than the human hand. Towards the end of 1923 (starting with a séance on 17 October 1923), when after the séance the medium, still in semi-trance was led to a sofa, large lights and nebulae started emanating from his neck, head, and chest. These phenomena did not cease even when the participants, leaving the medium lying down, started to depart from the room. On the contrary, they began to get stronger and from that time this phenomenon became increasingly frequent.

4. Lights which illuminated materialised apparitions: These resembled little electric lamps hidden in a veil or some transparent

material. They appeared close to the phantoms at various distances from the medium and would suddenly illuminate the phantom's face from the side, from above, or from below. They moved slowly and gave the impression of being somehow connected to the materialised phantoms.

Other groups of lights which illuminated materialised phenomena, and sometimes the participants as well, were those that appeared as if at the ends of invisible moving fingertips, mostly phosphorescent, smelling of ozone, more rarely radiant like jewels. If they produced vapours, they tended to be yellow-greenish, if they produced rays, these were milky and blue.

Non-phosphorescent luminous phenomena, radiant like jewels or burning metal, appeared separately, as well as lighting materialised figures, primarily their faces. If they had a clear shape they appeared as polygons, crosses, or small snakes and seemed to be independent, yet still gave the impression of being somehow connected to the phantoms. If they illuminated phantoms, they looked like a light source held in the hand.

An important feature of the phantoms was that their hands and fingers did not have the red tone of living hands when light shines through them.

Luminous phenomena with phosphorescent vapours represented a rich and varied range, from two or three which seemed to be connected to fingertips, to a mass of light spread over both hands, so strong that it illuminated the participants and the surrounding objects, as well as the phantom. They were sometimes so intense that they left phosphorescent and odorous (ozone or other) clusters long after the séance. In the light these appeared like damp, greasy spots (also emitting a smell), which disappeared after a few hours. These things happened both near to and far from the medium.

5. Lights which appeared a long way away (up to 5 metres) from the medium, mostly numerous multicoloured little lights which would arrange themselves suddenly into geometrical figures, shapes of flowers, etc. The dominant colours were green and yellow, but also red and blue, like miniature Bengal fires or like tiny electrical lights. They appeared rarely, independently, and did not seem to be related to any others.

6. Lights which served to emphasise the shape or expression of materialised phantoms (it would be difficult to describe their colour).

7. Lights observed on only a few occasions: They appeared to be highly charged, as if with electricity. They were pale blue, like an electric light, and tended to appear some 2 metres above the floor, towards

the end of the séance. They also seemed completely independent of others. Initially they were round or elliptical, misty but bright, without vapours, occasionally with a matt shining centre seen through the nebula which would then close over it again. This would happen a number of times, becoming increasingly brighter, and the light would disappear after reaching a climax. After such phenomena the medium would be totally exhausted. This group included streaks, triangles (red and yellow), and miniature columns (yellow with red spots), as well as flashes resembling miniature lightning, appearing suddenly for a moment. There were also little crosses with bluish light, and, on three occasions, what looked like a tiny moon, 10 cm in diameter, with parts of it disappearing, as if going through the phases of the moon. Other shapes resembled little pagan altars with green-blue vapours emanating from them; commas; miniature volcanoes; jewels; shining eyes; and shining snakes burning like molten metal.

8. The final group was that of various nebulae, which often served as the background to other luminous phenomena, but also appeared independently. They took on different shapes and appeared throughout the séance. They seemed to function like bridges between other luminous phenomena. They could be so strong that they filled the whole room like a mist. Sometimes they appeared where a phantom was about to materialise; they were usually grey-green and of varying density; they sometimes smelled of ozone, sometimes of other things. Usually they moved slowly and, on occasion, remained immobile. Their shapes were irregular, sometimes like flames which broke away from a fire, sometimes like human figures. They seemed to be of different temperatures, which could be very low. (In a footnote Okołowicz tells us that at a séance in September 1920, immediately afterwards, on a very hot evening, the temperature dropped by 10° C. He also speculates about the nebulae being part of the materialising and dematerialising process.)

Okołowicz also reports that on three occasions there appeared something resembling a ribbon of luminous lava, of a greenish colour, bent in the middle and looking as if it had luminous liquid inside it. It seemed flat, moved around the room, stretching at times to 0.5 metre, and ended by spilling onto a white sheet of paper, leaving a trace like spilled glycerine, which then disappeared from the paper.

Odours

Ozone (its nature confirmed by a number of scientists) was the most frequent odour occurring around Kluski, and was often associated with the luminous phenomena. As has already been mentioned, Kluski smelled of ozone when highly emotional, as well as before, during, and after séances, and the smell could persist for as long as 48 hours, especially if a séance left Kluski feeling confused. Emanations of this and other smells could also be so strong that whatever he came into contact with also became saturated with the same odour. The smell of ozone also appeared during experiments involving instruments such as a compass or a galvanometer. It was also apparent during attempts to mend an electrical lamp which stopped working, or when trying to start a clock which had stopped. The odour emanated not during the manipulation stage, but after success was achieved.

Apart from the ozone smell, other odours included animal smells, rotting flesh, sweat or dirty clothing. There were also pleasant smells such as of fruit, leaves, flowers or incense, not associated with any specific phenomenon, and smells associated with particular phantoms (e.g. disinfectant accompanying phantoms which appeared wounded or sick, or garlic and spices with some Eastern-looking apparitions). On one occasion (in April 1920), a participant asked for rose oil and a few minutes later he and his neighbours were sprinkled with rose oil of which they smelt for a long time. There was no rose oil anywhere in the apartment.

All the smells were concentrated in the medium and when he was lightly dressed or naked it was possible to tell that the smells came from his chest, head, hands, armpits, and sweat. He also absorbed smells, particularly alcohol, as well as strong foods and strong ambient smells (e.g. flowering lime trees or acacia). Such phenomena were quite frequent.

Materialisations

Animal apparitions

In 1924, Okołowicz published a paper on animal apparitions in *Zagadnienia Metapsychiczne* (No. 2); it is summarised below. Much of this information can also be found in an article by Barbara McKenzie (McKenzie 1926-7), who obtained it from Okołowicz.

Animal apparitions usually seemed to appear with people, and would not be illuminated but, rather, be perceptible by touch, hearing, and smell. However, there were also seen in the red light, ichneumon- or squirrel-like creatures, which would run around the table and up the participants' arms. Animal phantoms started to appear from the earliest séances but were not properly recorded due to the abundance of various phenomena.

The earliest was one which the participants named "Hirkil". It looked like a lion without its mane, was smelly, and insistently tried to lick everyone with a wet and prickly tongue. Neither the animal nor its keeper were wanted by the participants but they kept appearing over a number of months. Among the early apparitions was also a bird of prey, like a large hawk, which was photographed when it first appeared on 30 August 1919. Mrs McKenzie's account provides further details of this phenomenon, obtained from Okołowicz: Prior to the exposure, there was a whirring sound, like that of large unfurling wings, and slight blasts of wind. The sitting was held in the light of a red lamp, about 3 metres away from the medium, and in this light the participants could see the outlines of a grey moving mass, which was identified as a bird only after the plate had been developed.

Figure 3: *Materialisation of a bird*

Among the early apparitions was also the ape-like creature, described as the "primitive man" or "Pithecantropus". It had a light-brown hairy coat, a head full of tangled hair, and was in the habit of loudly smacking its lips. It first appeared in July 1919 and gradually became much clearer, probably because of the interest of the participants. It seemed stupid but friendly, and was annoying because of being too eager to please. It tried to imitate other phantoms in carrying out requests but did not understand them, for example, when phantoms were asked to bring something it would rush along with something unsuitable, or try to lift two participants in turn. When admonished, it would hide under the table and try to lick people with an enormous wet tongue. It was photographed three times between August and November 1919, but unfortunately the pictures were of very poor quality because the light came on too late. This phenomenon weakened gradually and by 28 November 1919 only fragments of it seemed to appear, so that there would be smacking in one corner, scratching in another, while one participant felt a hairy mass rub against him.

Formation of human apparitions

During the early period of Kluski's mediumship there were many partial materialisations. There were unfinished busts, hands with missing fingers or fingers hanging on, as well as apparitions which looked as if they had been made from cardboard or rags. The rarest materialisations were those that were smaller or larger than normal. There were more of them early on, usually exotic females, about half or a third of one of normal size. The artificial-looking phantoms were preceded by sounds like the rubbing of cardboard or fabric and the tearing of paper, but no trace of such objects was ever found.

Throughout Kluski's mediumship, there were what Okołowicz refers to as the "dark phantoms", the majority of which seemed to be an intermediate phase of the fully materialised ones. They seemed to have combined features, resembling the medium in their gait but with the lightness of touch of a young girl. Sometimes they seemed to divide into two, three, or more figures materialised to different degrees. Some seemed to be interested in the séance, others appeared aimless, wandering about and, for example, looking at the books as if they could see in the dark. They seemed to have their own concerns and personalities and sometimes seemed to argue among themselves, while some seemed to be looking out for particular participants.

Okołowicz also describes the formation of materialised form from light nebulae, creating floating and misty phantoms. These materialisations seemed to undergo continuous transformations and sometimes foreshadowed more substantial manifestations. Often visible after the séance, they were mostly greyish-green in colour, less often yellow and very rarely bluish, sometimes with a smell, but always mobile, scattering, and clustering again. Their mobility was very different from that of the passive movements such as smoke in a closed room or breezes caused by human movements. A rarer phenomenon would be nebulae with a clear human or animal shape. They would form in various ways, either from small nebulae or from nebulae caused by the ongoing light phenomena. This last kind of formation would be the easiest to see, and the phantoms would often leave traces of phosphorescent substance on the floor or furniture. This substance would disappear after a while.

Okołowicz gives a description of a typical materialisation in his account of the séance on 19 June 1922[6]:

> Suddenly, in a corner of the room (some 2 metres from the medium) a misty human shape appears. We see it clearly in the light of the red lamp. It is flowing, and moves through the furniture easily. It stops at the desk, 5 metres away from the medium and beyond the light of the red lamp, but it is still visible like a misty pole the height of a man. We can hear paper rustling and small objects being moved, the figure sometimes seems to bend over the desk. When there are stronger noises coming from the desk the medium trembles, otherwise he stays very quiet. After a moment the figure floats towards us, through the furniture without disturbing it. It suddenly stops close to a participant who feels the touch of a warm hand (which he cannot see) which puts a piece of paper in his hand. We at the same time observe only a flowing and immobile nebula, vaguely resembling a human shape, and a clearer and brighter piece of paper floating into the hand of the participant. The nebula suddenly disappears and a few seconds later we see it a metre away, by the wall, shadowed by the furniture, as if motionless. A moment later we have the impression that it is absorbed into the wall, and then it finally disappears.

At times the shape of the phantoms seemed to be filled by a number of different figures, creating an unpleasant and disturbing impression on most participants. The face would become a female or a male without for a moment losing its double character; sometimes there would even be three faces which seemed to be superimposed on each other, transparent like glass, yet seeming like flesh. The least mobile features were the eyesockets, which seemed to be shared. If one of the

---

[6] The reports are usually in the present tense and often from different points of view, clearly amalgamating observations by different witnesses.

participants tried to describe what they saw, that set of features seemed to form more clearly. The medium would always be disturbed by this phenomenon, trembling while it was happening and feeling nervous and physically exhausted after the séance.

Undoubtedly the medium's state and mood was reflected to some extent in the phantoms, and vice versa. The participants' expectations also influenced the appearance of the manifestations. A phantom would appear, not very clearly but, on approaching a person who recognised it with emotion, it would gradually become clearer both to that person and to others close by. On the other hand, on moving further away, it would lose some of its expressiveness and individuality for the other participants, as if the emotional "support" was involved in its creation. One of the many examples of such support comes from the séance on 12 February 1925, when a participant remembers a friend whose phantom appeared previously and observes the changes in the features of the apparition which had not seemed familiar a moment earlier. The face becomes slimmer and younger, a little moustache appears, and the face becomes that of his deceased friend. However, sometimes the participants also seem to have played a role even at the material level. At the séance on 22 March 1924 a participant's report (Stanisław Sedlaczek) states:

> I remember very clearly the head and as if the whole body, anyway down to the waist, of a young girl with a Japanese face. The face dead, as if made of plaster or heavily powdered, with very clear black eyebrows. A moment later, there is only the head, a yellow face of an old Japanese woman. Before this, participant No. 2 complains of "pulling" on the mouth and an unpleasant feeling around the eyes; at one point, it seems at the very moment of the appearance of the first Japanese woman, participant No. 2 falls asleep but is immediately woken by her neighbour. She then still complains about the unpleasant sensation around the mouth and eyes.

Formation of accessories

Among the factors affecting the nature and clarity of the phantoms' accessories, Okołowicz includes the presence of relevant objects nearby. If a séance took place in a room with lots of furniture and ornaments, and the participants' clothing was varied, the phantoms seemed to have no problem dressing themselves. They seemed to rub various objects prior to appearing, as if transforming the "raw material" into what was needed. It was very often observed that, for example, an officer's phantom would have a clearly detailed military cap but the uniform would be a blur, vaguely resembling what the medium was wearing at the time. However, when attention was paid to the uniform, the phantom seemed to "grow" one. When officers in Russian uniforms appeared, the officers present at the séance felt their epaulettes and buttons being rubbed, after which the phantoms' epaulettes and buttons would shine. Another example comes from the séance on 10 June 1924, when a participant felt her string of pearls being rubbed and then an exotic female phantom appeared (self-illuminating) with a large string of pearls. The impression was so strong that the owner of the pearls automatically checked whether her own pearls were still in place. When compared, the phantom's string of pearls turned out to be longer and the pearls larger. This "doubling" or "duplicating" was quite frequent, and most often involved Kluski's clothing as well as that of the participants. Phantoms also seemed to rub against the soft furnishings, and the clothing of all those present, particularly Kluski, showed signs of wear after a séance. Okołowicz found that his own clothing looked as if someone had brushed it with a very sharp brush and given it a violent beating. The fabric would become worn and threadbare. At one sitting (on 26 January 1925), the medium wore dark-red silk pyjamas which he had only worn two or three times previously, and wore for the first time at a séance. After the séance, the garment was found to be totally worn through in places, like a web. The phantoms would also use things present in the room, like spectacles or a straw hat, and respond to comments. On one occasion, a phantom took up the medium's comb and combed its abundant hair after the remark that its hair looked artificial.

Difficult to classify is the incident reported during the séance on 11 November 1922. The medium's fur coat, lying on the settee about 3 metres from the circle, suddenly started moving and jumping, and then the phantom of the "primitive man" emerged from it to run around the room, while the fur remained motionless where it had been.

Kinds of apparitions

1. Screen-illuminated human apparitions

Apparitions which illuminated themselves with the screen usually materialised partially and less clearly, appeared for a shorter period, sometimes had difficulty in moving, and most frequently came into contact with only some participants, very clearly avoiding others. At times some were impudent but, on the whole, they were polite and gentle. Others seemed to appear in order to persistently repeat the same activities, yet others seemed to have come to watch the phenomena with the participants. Some seemed to be visibly disappointed when they were not recognised or if they did not find among those present the people who recognised them previously as phantoms of deceased relatives or friends. Some, at times, had features which resembled the medium, especially when they appeared for the first time.

During the initial period, almost all phantoms were unexpected, in the sense that there was no attempt to induce a particular kind of phantom and no discussion of what might happen. The "primitive man" appeared quite unexpectedly and inexplicably. Phantoms of a worker and a gendarme at another séance might be related to the left-wing protests in Warsaw at that time, while an essay on a historical figure of an 18th-century female spy which Kluski was writing at the end of September 1920 might have influenced the apparition of an elderly lady with a very characteristic face and costume which appeared at the séances at IMI in Paris. Gradually, as some phantoms kept reappearing, they would become more life-like and differentiated, some repeating the same activities, such as the phantom of the Italian patriot Cesare Battisti (executed by the Austrians during the war), which first appeared at a séance in Italy but then kept manifesting at numerous séances, and whose behaviour was very similar on every occasion. Another set of phantoms who began to appear in June 1924 consisted of a number of polite Turks who seemed like a response to the prevailing political circumstances, when Poland and Turkey were trying to collaborate more closely and a Polish exhibition was being organised in Constantinople. Altogether, there had been about 200 different apparitions which illuminated themselves with the screen, however, many of them could be categorised as groups using the same "raw material", such as military men with their uniforms, exotic types, or a number of female types.

The phantoms, particularly the later ones, were highly respons-
ive to the participants' impressions. At a séance on 6 January 1925, a
participant who was attending for the first time (and who authored
the report) became worried about what he had read about the phenomena coming from Satan. He therefore started praying in his mind
and the phantom (of an old lady recognised as another participant's
mother) approached him and made the sign of the cross on his forehead, while a later apparition was that of a monk who seemed to pray
in Latin over him.

When dealing with phantoms of deceased persons, Okołowicz
defined as such only those recognised by participants who were prepared to sign a certificate to that effect. In total, 84 persons confirmed
recognition of 88 phantoms of deceased persons known to them.
About a quarter of them did not want their names or the names of the
phantoms published. The largest group among the phantoms was, not
surprisingly in view of the participants' backgrounds and the times, of
soldiers, mainly officers.

Okołowicz quotes a number of cases where the phantoms kept appearing for some time, even months, without being recognised, until
the right participant happened to attend (séance on 21 July 1924) and
confirmed its identity and close resemblance to the deceased person.
Another case of interesting interaction was that which took place at a
séance held in May 1924. Before the séance one of the participants, Mr
Stanisław M., told the story of a Mr Küster, whom he had known in
Volyn, and who was passionately interested in spiritualist phenomena.
Before his death he had declared to Mr M. that he would show himself
to him as a phantom at the earliest opportunity, and in fact was seen
in one of the manor houses in Volyn a year after his death, in daylight,
which was apparently confirmed by a number of people as well as Mr
M. After that, he appeared to Mr M. in dreams a number of times, also
a few days before the séance, when he told Mr M. that he would be at
the séance and would show himself to him. (Mr M. met Kluski only on
the day of the séance and was invited to the séance at that time). At the
séance in question "Mr Küster" appeared very clearly, and the description given by Mr M. corresponded fully to the phantom's appearance
(very distinctive, with a black patch over the right eye). This phantom
appeared twice at later séances demanding to see Mr M. (who attended only once). In total, it appeared 4 times. During the séance Mr M.
showed a strong tendency to become entranced and found it difficult
(as he said) to stay awake.

Okołowicz also reports three cases of phantoms of living persons; one (on 22 March 1924) frightened one of the participants, Ms JC, since the phantom was of her father with a strange confused expression in his eyes. She telegraphed the family, who lived in another town, and found out that her father was alive but had been very ill and at the time when the séance was taking place was unconscious with high fever.

2. Self-illuminating human apparitions

The second group of phantoms (which began to appear quite clearly towards the end of May 1923) was characterised by the perfection of their materialisations, which at times made them indistinguishable from living humans, as well as by their ability to maintain the state of full materialisation for quite a long time. These figures would be constantly visible, illuminating themselves with a light much stronger than the light of the screen. Their behaviour was always very dignified and solemn.

The most striking impression was their independence of the participants, who either dared not, or could not, treat them as the phantoms described earlier, to whom they directed requests and complaints. A significant feature of these phantoms was their total lack of similarity to the medium and the abundance of types, who differed very clearly from each other, although they had something in common in terms of their behaviour and the strength of the lights which emitted strong scents.

These phantoms had a deep, luminous expression in their eyes, and the ability to sense the intentions of the participants. Frequently they would react accurately to thoughts before the individual had a chance to articulate them. This was in contrast to some of the phantoms which illuminated themselves with the screen and which appeared not to realise that they existed and seemed to seek support, help, or information from the participants.

In total there were 45 such figures, the most frequent one being of an old lady carrying a cross, followed by one which came to be known as the Chaldean or Assyrian archpriest. Before these figures appeared in their own light, it could sometimes be seen that some dark figures approached the participants and strongly rubbed their backs and shoulders, something which came to be described as "the phantoms gathering strength." This massaging took place even during the early years of Kluski's mediumship, and was regarded by the participants as a kind of "distinction". However, it was not until the time when the phantom of the Chaldean priest began to appear that some participants began to feel the effects of these massages, which resulted in very intense physical and mental exhaustion of the person involved. It would be difficult to say how far these massages helped materialisations, but it was a fact that after them the phantoms were always very clear and visible. The phantoms always massaged the young and healthy, avoiding the exhausted, the old, and those who had been drinking alcohol before the séance

One particularly striking event took place at the séance on 2 August 1924:

> In the second part of the séance a phantom appeared which looked very much like the medium only younger, and illuminated itself with its own bluish light held in the left hand. Simultaneously, next to this phantom, there appeared a phantom of a young girl, visible in the light emanating from the first phantom. The two phantoms then moved towards the medium and we could clearly see one Kluski, sitting motionless and looking like a dead body, and another one, standing and looking alive.

Perhaps one might be reminded here of Kluski's first love, the girl who died young and whose death had a profound effect on him.

Mental phenomena

In many ways, all of the phenomena described above are mental. They involve the participants' desires and the phantoms' ability to fulfil them, often without these desires being expressed out loud. Activities involving the phantoms included the winding and setting of clocks, the bringing and moving of objects, or performing actions in a bid to be recognised, such as putting on glasses and making gestures, as well as making sensible comments when knocking in response to spoken alphabet (Okołowicz remarks wryly that this is sometimes in contrast to what was said by the participants, and points to the fact that the medium is a writer used to formulating his thoughts logically and clearly).

However, there were a number of events at the séances which seem to belong to a wider category of mental phenomena. They involved the physical activity of typing on the typewriter, but the knowledge which was demonstrated puts them in a somewhat different category. Thus, in June 1919 the typewriter wrote during a séance a longish sentence (in

Polish) beginning: *"Listen – the bells have stopped ringing..."* Nobody could see a connection between the message and anything that they were aware of, but three days later the famous French writer André Lichtenberg (who was then in Warsaw), giving (in French) a lecture on Poland's liberation, began the second half of it with a sentence with precisely that meaning. It was checked later that the writer was working on his speech at the time when the séance was taking place. The writer had never heard of Kluski and had never attended a séance.

At a séance on 8 June 1919 there was automatic writing on the typewriter, significant in that the meaning of the message was explained after the séance by a participant, Mr. Stefan Ok. A few minutes after the beginning of the séance those present became aware that, close to Mr St.Ok., there was a phantom trying to light itself, then steps were heard in the room and then the sound of the typewriter. After the séance, a sheet of paper was found in the typewriter, with the following words on it: *"But this is not the room in Brzeście – where are Terenia, Frania....?"* Mr St. Ok., having read the message, declared with surprise that it reminded him of his stay at the Brzeście country house which was the home of his cousin (by then deceased) and some nieces, two of whom were called Teresa and Franciszka (Terenia and Frania). He then added that nobody among the participants could have known about it. This particular participant met Kluski only a few hours before the séance.

During the séance on 23 November 1919 the typewriter wrote the sentence: *"I am the smile of balance, my poem of love and life has lasted epochs..."* but no corresponding text was ever found. At another séance in 1919 the typewriter wrote *"Józef in danger..."*. The next day the papers reported that the Marshal (Józef Piłsudski) had been in danger, finding himself unexpectedly under fire. The séance took place some 10 hours before the event.

And once, at a séance in May 1924, a new phenomenon, that of clairvoyance, never before exhibited by the medium, was recorded. Stefan Ossowiecki, the famous clairvoyant, was present at that séance.

A number of participants, worried about splashing paraffin on their clothes, took off their jackets and waistcoats and left them in the séance room on an armchair next to the desk. When after the séance Okołowicz was next to the semi-conscious medium lying on the settee, one of the participants came in to collect the clothes. However, as the room was dark, the participant had a problem trying to collect individual items without things like watches, cigarette cases etc., falling out of the pockets. The medium then, without moving and in a dreamy voice began to give instructions as to how collect each item, describing exactly what was in each pocket and to whom it belonged. The distance between the medium who was lying down and the things folded on the armchair was about 2.5 metres, and between him and the armchair was a large mahogany desk which would have blocked the view of the armchair even if there had been light in the room.

Okołowicz also describes an occasion when an unusual form of communication took place between the medium and the participants. In May 1922 a number of friends gathered in Kluski's apartment with the intention of holding a séance. However, Kluski was not at home. While waiting for his return it was decided to hold something like a séance in his study, in order to try and communicate with the medium regardless of where he might be at that time. Places were taken around the table, a chain of hands was formed and after turning off the light the participants began wishing together for contact with Kluski. During this sitting some knocks and rustles were heard. After 10 minutes the séance was interrupted and the participants moved to another room (among the participants were Dr T. Sokołowski and Dr J. Guirard). After a few minutes Kluski arrived and in an agitated voice asked, "What have you been doing here?" When the situation was explained to him, he said that about 30 minutes earlier, when he was having supper at a friend's house, knocks and noises were heard on the table, and then one of the hard-boiled eggs began to move so violently on the plate that it seemed about to fall off onto the table. Okołowicz adds that none of the family or the guests knew where Kluski was before his arrival.

Automatic writing

At the end of 1919 and the beginning of 1920 there were relatively fewer materialising séances and more automatic writing ones. These were first tried towards the end of July 1919 and were successful from the beginning. They were also less exhausting for the medium, who preferred them, and left behind evidence in the form of various conversations and messages written in different handwriting. However, the dominance of automatic writing seemed to have a negative effect on the richness of the materialising séances, which then became of poorer quality.

Automatic writing started with the medium sitting in full light in the evening, holding a pencil to paper without resting his elbow on the table. A moment later the pencil would start moving, while the medium would become slightly confused. The writing was initially large and clumsy, but it quickly developed as the medium's hand was allowed to operate in a normal position. The results were good, with clear writing unlike the medium's, and with differences between handwriting styles and attitudes to the subjects. In some ways, this resembled the emergence of phantoms, initially similar to the medium and then becoming more individualised. To start with, Kluski was against keeping the messages, preferring to destroy them immediately after the séance, hence there were very few samples from the early period.

After a few months' trials, a system was established with the medium sitting next to a light which shone on his hands and the paper, while the participant(s) sat next to him. It looked as if he was writing normally until you looked closely and saw that he was in a light trance. When the writing stopped he would become conscious. When he wanted a break he had to move the paper and pencil beyond his reach, otherwise he seemed to become a passive tool of whatever was controlling the writing and might write dozens of pages without being aware of it. This was all the more remarkable as, when conscious, Kluski would get tired when writing by hand and would normally use the typewriter. He would try not to read the messages unless they were of general interest (he used glasses for writing, but not for reading).

Initially, participants would become involved and would comment, but it was realised that things worked better with just one person, otherwise everyone would try to participate, including the "presences", who seemed to be trying to grab the pencil. Participants thus started to take it in turns, with those not wanted leaving the room and trying to think of something else. The medium's state of health affected the handwriting, which could be shaky, but not so much the content. Subjects would be expressed clearly and simply by different individualities, rather like a social conversation, with many "presences" appearing for the first time and usually claiming to be deceased persons known to the medium or the participants. Since most of this writing was very personal, Okołowicz mainly relied on the opinions of the participants, who overwhelmingly felt that the handwriting and the contents of the messages were undoubtedly those of the deceased persons. He was planning another book based on these séances (it does not seem to have been written), but at that time the material was not fully documented, needing further confirmation and verification. At that point, about 40 people had taken part, and about 150 entities, using different handwriting and different styles of expression, allegedly communicated.

In rough percentage terms, Okołowicz estimated that about 20% of the messages came from entities who claimed to appear at the physical séances; others claimed to have lived hundreds of years previously, some claiming to be guardians of the séance participants. The handwriting would then become similar to that of the individuals involved, although the content, both subject and style, would be very different. About 25% of the handwritten messages were recognised as the handwriting of deceased persons known to the sitter but not to the medium, with the content also being appropriate for the deceased. There were also unidentified, one-off communicators, as well as contemporary deceased entities unknown to the participants or the medium, who had never attended the séances but who could be identified later on the basis of the content and the handwriting. Perhaps most interestingly, about 3% were identified, by the writing, as being living persons not present but asleep at the time. In this latter case, the communication usually took the form of a dialogue between a participant at the séance and the entity. Apparently it was often confirmed that the correspondent "dreamt" the conversation.

The messages came not only in Polish but in Italian, German, French, Czech and Russian. There were also about a dozen in Turkish (in Turkish alphabet), two in Arabic, one in Sanskrit, and one in a Hindu dialect, (these all in the Latin alphabet). Kluski was fluent in Italian and Russian, and had a fair knowledge of German and French, but nobody there knew the other languages, which were identified by experts.

Unfortunately there are only two reports of automatic writing with a little more detail available to us. One is Count Juliusz Potocki's account of his conversation with his deceased relatives, published by Geley in *L'Ectoplasmie at la Clairvoyance*, which involves, not unexpectedly, recognition, delight, and strong emotions. The other is an account by Dr Antoni Czubryński in an unpublished manuscript on the *Supernormal States in Saints*,[7] given here in translation:

---

[7] Dr Czubryński was a psychical researcher and a free-thinking scholar in the field of religious studies; his unfinished manuscript *Supernormal States in Saints: A study in parapsychology and religion*, 1934-1946, was passed to me by the late Dr Roman Bugaj. Since in another passage there is also a literal quotation from the same communicator (to the effect that afterlife is not at all peaceful!), I assume that the account is probably based on contemporaneous transcript or notes.

One of the séances which made me think a lot involved the talented medium Teofil Modrzejewski. It took place on 8 August 1939 at 17:45 in his apartment at Królewska in Warsaw. A sheet of paper was on the table, the medium sat on a chair and I sat on his right to make sure that the paper should not slide away during the writing. The medium went into a trance quickly and easily and started writing with a pencil. I wanted to get in touch with Andrzej Niemojewski[8] on certain scientific matters which became important for us only after his death, because we never talked about them while he was alive, or only in most general terms. Apart from this, I was curious how far the Christian view would apply after death. I was not concerned with any spiritistic or other suppositions; I was only interested in the results and would form an explanatory hypothesis only on their basis. The medium began to write easily and quickly, in the handwriting of the deceased, but both in this and the next message the views expressed by Andrzej Niemojewski somehow did not at all fit with the freethinking opinions which he espoused and promoted in life. The handwriting was undoubtedly his, but his spirit was changed: it was clerical. We might suppose that truly it was he who was speaking, but his arguments had been distilled through the filter of the pious mentality of the medium, who censored them appropriately before committing them to paper. At that time this seemed to me like the most likely hypothesis. One might also suppose that the medium drew something from me and from himself, since he knew Andrzej Niemojewski personally, the latter having participated in séances when alive, and thus a mediumistic message was created which had nothing to do with the deceased A.N. However, the following fact spoke against this hypothesis: in his message A.N. used the Aramaic words "lek kulechi" – "it came to pass" from the Gospel of St John XIX 30, which corresponds to the Greek "telestai", and Latin "consummatum est," and in Hebrew would be expressed as "kullah." I was not familiar with this expression and it was only after the séance that I searched for it in the Hebrew dictionary of W. Gesenius. However, this was a Hebrew form, and the Aramaic form is not given in this dictionary,

---

[8] Andrzej Niemojewski (1864-1921); lawyer, poet and writer, expert on religious studies, social activist and an anti-clerical freethinker, imprisoned in 1911 for his antireligious publications. He published his impressions of sittings with Kluski (using the pseudonym Bogumił for Kluski) in his book *Dawność a Mickiewicz* in 1921.

not in the form given by A.N. One could hypothesise that I had seen it somewhere and had a visual memory of it. But since it was not given either in the Hebrew or Aramaic form of the dictionary, and since I was not familiar even with the Hebrew form "kullah" and had to look for it in the New Hebrew translation published by the British Bible Society, any hypotheses as to the words being brought to the surface from my memory by the medium must be rejected. Even less likely is the supposition that the medium might be familiar with this expression, since he had nothing at all to do with this subject. The only remaining and simplest hypothesis seems that the words came from the deceased. As to the strange change of views in the deceased from freethinking to pious, I explained this to myself as a mental amalgamation of the ideas of the deceased with those of the medium, with the latter being dominant and exercising censorship.

I held on to this auxiliary hypothesis, for want of something better, for a few years. After the message from A.N. there followed other messages at these séances, from people whom I never called. One was my father, and there were others, with their authentic handwriting, which the medium could not have been familiar with, and even if he was, could not have used it. Neither could I – a skilled artist may be able to copy someone's handwriting from a sample, but that is not the same as writing at length in someone else's handwriting.

But this was not the end. In his message, my father greeted me using a nickname he had for me when I was a child, which I had completely forgotten and which would be very inappropriate in relation to an adult. This confirmed me in my hypothesis that I was dealing with my deceased father. It was not only the handwriting, but his manner of speaking, his jocular-whimsical tone.

Altogether I had the impression as if a door had been opened through which other characters were trying to push in, who had not been called or invited, in order to make contact with me even briefly, in one or two sentences. Some asked bluntly what did I want with the dead and was I dead as well.

One could not call the medium's name since that would immediately wake him up. I was allowed to copy, and even photograph the messages, but I was not allowed to take them outside the medium's apartment.

The phantoms demanded that the originals be destroyed, apparently not wanting any links to remain between the two worlds.

Among the phantoms was one who began by greeting me and asking to be invited to our "feast" – as she gracefully put it, as if in the style of Plato ("Symposion" – a feast). The handwriting allowed me to guess who the person was, since I was in correspondence with her some years previously. This was a lady whom I knew socially for a while, but with time we no longer moved in the same circles, which often happens with acquaintances. We were parted by time, space, preoccupations, although nothing went wrong between us. On receiving the message I concluded that she was no longer alive, but did not know how and where she died. I also did not know to whom to turn for such information and, to tell the truth, it did not seem like an urgent matter to find out these details.

Finally, 8 years and 3 months from that séance, I accidentally met a mutual acquaintance whom I had not seen for a long time. From that person I learned that the lady in question escaped abroad during the war and was now living in England. This amazed me: a living person made contact in a mediumistic message in her own handwriting. How was that possible?"

The author then speculates on the phenomenology and dynamics of this situation, and expresses profound regret for not having tried to establish the contactee's circumstances at the time.

Experiments

A number of accounts exist of experiments involving magnets and electrical equipment. They tend to confirm the same effect, i.e., that Kluski was able (but not on every occasion), by waving his hands, to make the needle of a compass deviate in either direction to varying degrees, sometimes slightly, and sometimes so violently that it would make a complete revolution. Okołowicz tells us that, during experiments on 21 September 1921, compass needles responded to feet as well as hands, while the forearm had the strongest effect. Proximity of buttocks also produced success, while knees, ears, forehead, and tongue had no effect at all. More importantly, even though they tried to maintain the same conditions, the movements of the needles were different every time Kluski came close to them, as if he was emitting uneven, irregular waves of whatever influenced the needles. In another context, Okołowicz makes the same comment about the phenomena in general; they also seemed to come in irregular waves, weaker and stronger.

He also describes experiments with a galvanometer undertaken on 16 and 23 September 1921 by Count du Bourg de Bozas who wanted to test Kluski for electrical effects. The medium would sit at a table some 4 metres away from the galvanometer, holding a connector in his right hand, and holding his other hand above a zinc plate connected to the other connector at the height of at least 15 cm. The zinc plate was in addition covered with a thick and large book for better insulation. The tests were successful, although exhausting, and demonstrated to the Count's satisfaction that Kluski acted as a conductor of an invisible current, a "fluid", of which photographic evidence was obtained (taken when the needle of the galvanometer moved).

Figure 4: *Experiment with galvanometer*

However, in the opinion of Okołowicz, what they photographed was a materialisation of what Kluski imagined they hoped to see, showing something, a "substance", that bore no resemblance to anything produced either at the séances or in everyday life. There follows a description of what happened to electrical equipment in Kluski's presence, since this was a related situation.

Outside the séances, the table lamp would often go out when the medium and others needed light for reading or writing, and another lamp would light itself in another corner. When everyone moved to that light, it would go out and the other one would come on. Sometimes this would keep on happening until they gave up. Examination of the equipment showed no faults. The best way of dealing with it seemed to be to leave the room for a while, or to pay no attention to the equipment and it would eventually work properly again. Another way of dealing with the problem was for the medium to stroke the cable, thinking about removing the obstacle/insulation, while another person turned the switch. When it worked and the light did come on, the medium's hands and his whole body would emit a strong smell of ozone for a while.

Polish researchers also experimented with trying to get the medium to affect photographic film directly (thoughtography). Such experiments were undertaken twice in December 1921, with the medium lying down and applying the film to his forehead and willing his visions to be transferred to the film. The film was developed immediately and contours of figures could be made out, but the films were destroyed in error.

The creation of paraffin wax moulds was an aspect of experiments undertaken with Kluski which continues to feature largely in various accounts and explanations, and for this reason deserves a separate section.

3.5. A range of séances

The excerpts and summaries from séance reports presented in this chapter are given in chronological order, and are aimed at reflecting the range and the changes in the nature of the phenomena which took place during the period of Kluski's reported mediumship. Okołowicz is the author of most of the reports published in his book, but quite a few contributions are by other sitters, and this is also reflected here.

While Okołowicz quotes full reports of the "official" séances where phenomena were produced, he also refers to some which are not given in full because of their similarity to the ones already given, as well as unsuccessful ones where nothing of note happened. The latter cannot have been very numerous, judging by the spread of the dates, but there certainly were a few, most notably the totally unsuccessful one held at the request of Mme Geley (who had arrived from Paris to attend her husband's funeral) after the death of Dr Geley in an air crash in 1924. Everyone was sad, the medium could not enter the trance state, and all that happened was the appearance of weak little lights at the end of the room. All the numbered "official" reports are signed by the listed participants, and provide dates, times, duration, and the conditions of the séance. What is striking is the similarity of impressions which runs through the various witness statements.

1. In chronological order, the first report, by Norbert Okołowicz, describes parts of a séance which is unique because of its violence and, as its author remarks, is comparable to some of the séances with Indridi Indridason, the famous Icelandic medium. It took place on 24 August 1919. The participants were eight in number apart from Kluski, and all were male.

After an unsuccessful attempt to obtain photographs, when no phantoms appeared, the medium left the room and came back extremely annoyed about something. The phenomena which followed had never been observed previously. There were no lights, just kinetic phenomena which became so violent that people feared for their safety, although nobody was hurt. Immediately after turning off the light, in the corner, about 1.5 metres from the medium, a wooden column (weighing ca 20kg) noisily broke away from the surrounding furniture, rose to the ceiling and hung there hitting the ceiling for a few moments. It then fell suddenly between two participants (Okołowicz being one of them), but without hurting them. At almost the same time, a small easel rose to the ceiling and fell with a deafening noise at the same point as the column. This lasted about ten to twelve minutes and was so unnerving that it was decided to stop the séance. The medium was not in a trance and was quiet. After a break, during which the furniture was put back, the phenomena started again. They seemed even stronger and highly dispersed, so that violent moving and shaking of the furniture was taking place all over the room, while small objects were being thrown about. Concern arose, not only for the participants but for the furniture, and after about ten minutes the séance was stopped. The medium was still not entranced, and asked about people's safety.

Another sitting was started with the light turned off, all agreeing to try a coordinated attempt to calm things down. However, the phenomena started almost immediately and were just as violent. Even though the participants had agreed to act in concert, each in fact turned to his own remedy; one praying aloud, another using Indian or Arabic incantations, while the rest spoke various calming words aloud. All this seemed to aggravate the violence and things began to levitate, as if threatening those present. Mr C.'s chair rose jerkily about 2 m with him sitting in it and fell down violently, but slowed just before landing and thus did not hurt him. Finally, a carafe with red wine standing next to the fireplace rose to the ceiling and fell to the floor, breaking into pieces. The séance was stopped immediately, and in the light it was found that the carafe was broken in such a way that a third of it, together with the base, looked as if it had been cut off with a knife, while the upper part was broken into tiny pieces. Chairs had been moved or overturned. There were no other phenomena, and it seemed as if the furniture had come alive.

After a twenty-minute break, it was suggested that an automatic writing séance be held, and Kluski agreed. He took a pencil and wrote a few words, but the pencil broke into little pieces. A new pencil was given to him, but it also broke. This happened again and again, as if some invisible force was destroying them. When nearly all the available pencils had been used up, the participants tried a special celluloid pencil, so thick and strong that it could not be broken even by a strong man. However, as soon as the medium took it up with the fingers of his right hand and touched the paper, the pencil broke violently in half (all in full light). The séance was stopped and a new supply of pencils was found. The attempt to write was made again after half an hour, and by that time the medium was much calmer. The writing was mainly in Russian, and was directed against the participants. It was extremely vulgar and full of snide comments, as if trying to be malicious towards everyone in turn. Gradually the form of expression and the content became calmer and began to sound like a serious discussion.

2. Report of séance conducted on 30 August 1919. Part of this report was included by Geley in his *L'Ectoplasmie et la Clairvoyance*. Apart from having a detailed description of the "primitive man", it is very typical of the early séances in terms of other apparitions. It was also the occasion when the well-known photograph of the materialised bird was taken (Fig.3).

There were in fact three sittings during that evening and night, all taking a similar course. Not counting the medium, those present included four female and four male participants. The excerpts given here are from the second sitting, aimed at taking photographs, which began at 00:15 hours and lasted until 2:45, and the third sitting, which lasted from 4:00 until 4:15 and also involved taking a photograph.

After a few minutes, those present become aware of rustles, crackling, and lights. When the medium asked verbally for the apparition's permission to be photographed, there were three knocks, indicating agreement. The medium asked the apparition to indicate readiness to be photographed by knocking four times. At that time the simultaneous presence of a number of apparitions could be discerned. The first to let itself be known was an apparition familiar from previous séances. It was a human-sized creature covered in rustling skin, very hairy, with abundant hair and beard, whose behaviour was reminiscent of an animal or a primitive human. Instead of speech it produced sounds of gobbling, babbling, and chomping teeth, in an attempt to communicate with those present. When called upon to do so it would allow itself to be stroked or would stroke and lightly scratch with its claws. It obeyed the medium's instructions, taking care when dealing with the participants, in contrast to the previous séances, during which it manifested a degree of savagery. The most characteristic phenomenon was the persistent licking of those sitting in the circle on their faces and hands, as if this activity was particularly enjoyable. All those present objected, since they found it unpleasant. Instructions for the tasks to be carried out by the creature were given not only verbally but also mentally.

The next to make itself known was the apparition, also known from previous séances, referred to as "Karol". This apparition greeted Colonel Okołowicz by hitting him three times on the hand. It then communicated using the alphabet (i.e., a knock would indicate the required letter when the alphabet was spoken aloud). Asked when it had lived it said "13 years ago". It did not agree to be photographed, saying "another time". Asked for a reason, it answered, "he cannot", repeating this comment a number of times and thus indicating that the statement concerned the medium. The response to the medium's curt remark "this rascal is fibbing" was what sounded like clapping a number of times, and the medium experienced this as quite strong blows on his head, back, and hands. After an interval caused by this event, when asked how many other apparitions were there apart from him, the apparition said "many". Asked finally what the name was of the apparition of the "primitive man" which appeared simultaneously with it, it replied that it did not know. Immediately afterwards there appeared consecutively two female apparitions. These were small faces together with the beginnings of a torso. The first one was recognised from previous séances as an Indian woman from Calcutta, "Rheri", with whom one needed to communicate in English. Then four knocks were heard. After pouring magnesium into the magnesium lamp, the electric red lamp standing on the desk went out by itself, untouched by anyone. Ensign D. then took a photograph, and the light came on by itself. After a short break caused by lighting the magnesium light, crackling and rustling came from behind the medium, indicating movement of furniture. At about 02:45 hrs the séance was stopped, and those present realised that the table and a wooden column, together with a candlestick, had been moved above the heads of the medium and the participants, and placed in the middle of the room close to the camera. It was also found that the settee had been moved closer to the participants.

After the film was developed it was found that the visible part of some hairy head closely resembled the apparition known as "the primitive man". The phenomenon in the second photograph was the figure of a bird, which had never been seen in Kluski's apartment before or after the séance.

In *Psychic Science* (McKenzie 1926-27, 17:18), in her article *Materialized Animal Apparitions*, Mrs Hewat McKenzie described her experience of the presence of the "primitive man":

The only animal, according to Ocholowicz [sic], which seemed to be able to act independently of a keeper was the "pithecanthropos" or great ape, and I can certainly certify to this, having, in 1922, seen the creature lift the luminous slate and with it illumine and show its face quite clearly, and then, while carrying the slate, proceed to the other side of the circle, where I saw its jaw and shoulder illumined from behind in the same way. No other apparition accompanied it.

3. The séance on 17 March 1920, again at Kluski's Warsaw apartment, witnessed by two female and three (originally six) male participants, includes much information about various aspects of the formation of the apparitions. It involved three sittings, and excerpts from two of them are summarised here. At the second sitting (which began at 00:15 hrs), the screen lying on the table rose suddenly in the air and lit a clearly distinguishable human face, which resembled the face of the medium, close to the heads of the participants. This face appeared again, but now above the middle of the table and above the heads of the participants. It was similar to the previous one, but differed from it by having an unruly abundant head of hair and a trailing beard. At that time the medium did not have a beard, only a moustache. It was seen again for the third time after a while, still higher and further from the medium, with the hair but without any facial hair. Then unclear voices and whisperings could be heard, which sounded as if they were coming from the throat.

At the third sitting, which began an hour later: The medium, interested in the participants' reports of the phenomena during the second séance, decided not to go into a trance but to participate in observing the phenomena. A few minutes after the beginning of the séance the red light went out by itself. [...]

The screen suddenly rose in the air and, suspended there, began to approach the participants in sequence and to light in detail the apparitions of four faces which appeared consecutively. Between the appearance of these faces, one could hear rustles and knocks and see various little lights. The first observed apparition was formed shapelessly, as if out of a piece of white fabric in which the eyes and the nose were irregularly located, and thus barely resembled a human face. When those present demanded a clearer face, one immediately appeared, better formed but giving the impression of a cardboard cut-out. The upper part of this face was motionless and, on the lower part of the face, one could clearly see a thin red mouth and the tip of the tongue sticking out and moving quickly across. The third face seemed to be Chinese, similar to the two previous faces. One could see the slanting eyes and abundant black moustache, but it did not at all look like a living human face. [...]

The fourth face, a woman's face, illuminating itself with the screen held by a hand invisible to those present, approached each participant when requested, as did previous ones. Some participants had the impression that the face kept changing. First it was the face of an older woman, then suddenly it became young. When the medium, again in a very rough manner, demanded that the face should come close to his face, blows could be heard again, as if someone was punishing the medium by hitting him on the back and head, while the apparition came close to the medium's face, almost touching it. This face showed itself to the other participants very clearly from every side, so that all those present could distinguish its features in detail. It was a large, full face, with lively black eyes, prominent cheekbones, and strongly flushed. While these faces were showing themselves one could also hear some rustles and sounds coming from behind the medium, as if fabric, paper, cardboard, etc., were being rubbed against each other.

After the apparition of the faces there appeared, first close to the medium and then above the heads of the participants, very intense lights achieving the size of a hen's egg and at times shining with a brilliant green-silver light. After a moment one of these lights was seen, over a period of a dozen or so seconds, illuminating strongly the shape of a hand with dark contours, as if from the inside. From these lights, floating in the air, came what looked like shining smoke, accompanied by a very strong smell of ozone, which the participants smelled until the end of the séance. Some of the participants were touched by what seemed like a shining, flowing stream which over a period continued to shine on the hands, hair, and faces which it touched. The little fires, which kept appearing in increasing numbers, started to travel through the medium and come out of him. When Colonel Okołowicz requested that the lights should travel through him, one of the large bright lights passed through his back and came out of his chest in a manner visible to all present. At the same time, he experienced a light touch first on his back and then on his chest. Then, at the request of that participant, the light appeared above the middle of the table, passed through it, with a slight crackle, was seen under the table, and then, again after a crackle, on the surface of the table.

The screen, previously lying motionless on the table, suddenly turned bright side up, and against its background there appeared first a small hand, immediately followed by a pair of intertwined hands. These hands looked like the hands of a dummy, but with the temperature of a human body. The little finger of one of these hands was partly broken off and hung on a thread. These hands allowed the medium and the participants to clasp and shake them, and even to pull them towards themselves. However, when they all firmly clasped the hands and the medium cried out "light!", the hands dissolved without a trace, and after a moment appeared again against the screen. When those present later expressed their displeasure at the hands not being similar to human hands and unpleasant to touch, albeit feeling alive, they found a warm hand in the middle of the table, which allowed itself to be held, responding with friendly clasps. This warm hand, smaller than the hand of the medium, was either the right or the left hand, depending on which hand was extended to it by the participants. When one of the participants enquired as to why it had no ring, the next time he touched it he felt a ring. The hand then moved the ring along the finger and put it for a moment on the finger of Colonel Okołowicz but immediately took it off. It then put the ring on the screen and visibly moved it around it, allowing everyone to touch the ring, but when an attempt was made to remove it, the fingers moved the ring towards the hand and disappeared together with it. At the request of those present, the medium voiced the request, "bring me an apple". Immediately afterwards an apple appeared, with a large stem and leaves, as if freshly picked. The apple moved into the middle of the screen, and then everybody experienced a very strong smell of apples. When a female participant expressed doubt regarding the apple, she suddenly felt someone firmly pressing an apple to her face. When the medium demanded, "bring me a comb", at that moment a comb appeared on the screen, and rising, began to comb the medium's moustache and the hair of the participant sitting close to him. When asked, "where did the comb come from?", the answer given by knocking was, "from the dressing table." At the same time there were also appearances of the phantom known from the previous séances as the "primitive man." Then single little fires, streaks of light, rustles, and knockings coming from opposite corners of the room were experienced. Some 10 minutes before the end of the séance the red electric light came on by itself, and all the manifestations continued with the same intensity until the end of the séance in spite of the sudden turning on of the light. The séance was stopped at 02:30 hrs, by switching on the ceiling light. What was particularly worthy of attention during the third sitting was the fact that, in a number of cases, when the medium expressed a categorical order, the appearing faces moved close to his face and the faces of his neighbours, and moved the screen in such a way that the medium could look at them from all sides. (The medium's sight was very poor, but he never wore spectacles during the sittings.) When the medium expressed his orders very harshly, he would be hit, as if by someone standing behind him, on the head, hands, and back (once even very forcefully with a big and heavy album on the head). However, the apparitions continued to obey the medium and moved close in accordance with his wishes, so close as has never been observed at any previous séances.

Immediately after the sittings, a search for the apple was initiated throughout the apartment, but it was not found anywhere. However, on a small dressing table standing about 5 m from where the séance took place, a comb was found, very much like the one shown against the screen during the séance.

When three participants were later leaving the apartment, together with the medium, they saw, in the dark staircase corridor, above the head of the medium and behind him, little fires. And when they were saying goodbye to him in the weakly lit street, they observed in his open mouth what looked like a tiny electric light with a silver-green tone. It appeared and disappeared a number of times. (Signatures of the participants follow)

4. At the séance on 24 April 1922, with Richet and Geley acting as controllers, Kluski sat completely naked and, in spite of the room being very cold, he was warm, sweating and exhausted by the end of the hour-long sitting. There was the usual range of phenomena summarised by Geley, whose account is quoted by Okołowicz, who adds two items of information: that one of the participants had the impression that the apparitions first materialised naked and then attempted to provide themselves with clothing; and that the whole body of the medium was covered with bleeding and scratches after the séance, disappearing without a trace by the next day.

5. Summary of report by Alfons Gravier, a well-known architect and member of the Polish SPR, of a séance held on 26 October 1922 in Warsaw, from 22:20 until 23:15 (very typical of that period).

Participants take their places in the following order: Franek Kluski (medium), on his left, in that order, Mme Missiuro, Mjr de Mazarat (French), Mjr Missiuro, Colonel Okołowicz, Dr J. Guirard, A. Gravier and General A. Bieliński who links to the medium with his right hand.

On the table was a container with paraffin wax melted in boiling water and a shining screen.

After the main light was turned off, the red lamp remained on for the apparitions themselves to turn it off. After about a quarter of a minute groups of little lights appeared, and the persons sitting closest to the medium began to feel touches. (Light phenomena appeared even prior to the turning off of the red lamp). Suddenly the red lamp was turned off in an invisible manner since no one saw a hand approaching the lamp, yet the lamp plug was in the socket.

Then a number of very clear and beautiful phantoms appeared. One of them was a figure of a woman of great beauty, visible down to her waist. The apparition seemed to light itself as if with a precious jewel held in her left hand above her head. The light was the colour of moonlight and it looked as if the phantom was holding a piece of the moon. The hand of the apparition was bare and the arm covered only in beautifully draped muslin, which seemed to be the clothing of the apparition as a whole.

A number of other phantoms appeared in similar circumstances. One of them lifted the luminous screen from the table and illuminated itself with it. However, the screen, which had been in use for some time, gave poor light. Against this screen three further dark phantoms appeared later, their silhouettes clearly visible.

At one point the luminous screen was lifted in the air and used to show that the paraffin container was no longer on the table. The container had imperceptibly been lifted from the table and carried, without any mishap, onto a chair positioned behind Mme Missiuro. Apart from apparitions there were groups of lights, some of them giving the impression of being threaded onto a stiff wire. At one point they formed a cross which floated above the table. There were also many vapours made of light, which lit a very large area above the table.

The séance was interrupted when the medium became agitated, breathing very violently, and seeming to choke.

After the séance, three paraffin moulds were found. They were placed, during the séance, on the hands of Mme Missiuro, General Bieliński and Mr Gravier. All of these were moulds of hands. The largest was given to Mr Gravier. This mould represented a female left hand, with the thumb under the palm. This mould was amazingly like the hand of Mr Gravier's aunt, whose phantom appeared very frequently at the séances at which he was present.

After this séance, Messrs Franek Kluski, Guirard, Okołowicz and Gravier sat down to a séance of automatic writing. This experiment kept being interrupted by the constant extinguishing of lamps by invisible phantoms. It gave the impression of an attempt being made to interrupt the writing by systematically extinguishing those lamps which were needed, and turning on those not needed, and it would continue to do this when the participants lit those wanted and extinguished the unwanted ones. This phenomenon affected three lamps placed in various distant locations in the room, and lasted about 15 minutes. Information obtained at the written séance was personal and for this reason is not quoted in this report. (Signatures of participants follow).

6. The séance on 26 December 1922 was reported by Okołowicz and involved a number of new phenomena. The apparitions did not, as previously, gather around the medium or the participants, but nearly all appeared simultaneously in the middle of the room, some 2 metres from the circle of participants.

One of the apparitions (a man in civilian clothes), before taking a few steps towards the opposite corner of the table, lighting itself with a screen on the way, changed into a saluting Polish officer wearing a cap and coat. Just before its appearance, and before the disappearance of the previous one, the clicking of heels and clashing of spurs could be heard.

When during that séance one of the participants, Teodor R., sang a well-known song in a low voice, a barely visible apparition began to whistle an accompaniment. Before the end of the séance there appeared (seen six times on previous occasions) the dancing phantom of a bald, bearded old man, whom Teodor R. recognised immediately as a harmless crazy Jew whom he used to know in Warsaw some twenty years previously.

Okołowicz adds that at one of the automatic writing séances in 1919, some words were written which were incomprehensible to those present, with the request to have them repeated to Teodor R. who was not present on that occasion. He was told these words after two days and he declared, with surprise, that they reminded him very clearly of a situation dating to twenty years earlier, when these very words were spoken to him by a mentally ill Jew, whom at that time he did not yet know personally. According to Teodor R, there were no witnesses to this encounter, and he never related it to anyone. The medium and the participants only learnt of the existence of this mentally ill person and the encounter when told by Teodor R.

7. The séance on 6 June 1923 seems to have been the first occasion featuring the new kind of self-illuminating phantom. It took place in Kluski's study at about 23:30 and lasted for over an hour.

After the typical beginning of noises and lights, larger lights appeared high above the heads of the participants, the size of a human hand. After a moment, they disappeared leaving behind them lightly glowing nebulae, and at the same time one of the participants declared that a phantom was standing behind him, continuously touching him and rubbing itself against him. Two other participants reported touches as well.

At the same time loud noises came from behind the medium, as if someone was hitting the wall and the wardrobe standing next to it with a stick. At that point a novice participant asked whether the phenomena could rise to the ceiling, and was told that such phenomena were quite frequent. A few moments later the knock of a stick on the ceiling was heard, and then noisy knocking on the wooden rings right under the ceiling, from which hung the curtain behind the backs of the medium and the participant who asked the question.

As the medium remained calm during this series of phenomena, no attempt was made to quieten the noises. After those passed, the momentary silence was interrupted by a knock as if a heavy wooden stick had been thrown into the centre of the room. After the séance, it was found that all of the three walking sticks which stood in the corner of the room behind the curtain were lying in disarray in the middle of the room.

This was followed by rustlings again, the touching of those present by some invisible figures, and the appearance of lights, similar to the previous ones, with the exception of one large luminous ball floating just under the ceiling and shining so brightly that it lit up the ceiling and the upper part of the walls. This ball disappeared shortly after without any sound, and the participants noticed that, between the medium and the participant next to him, there formed a large misty-white figure, quite clearly visible in the light of the red lamp which continued to shine. Simultaneously one of the participants declared that someone was covering his head with a veil so that at times he could not see anything. Another participant observed that the red light kept shining for a long time yet normally it would go out by itself a few minutes after the beginning of the séance, and when yet another participant expressed the wish to see apparitions which light themselves with the screen, the white phantom disappeared, and a few moments later the red lamp went out. Noises could be heard in the proximity of the medium. After that a number of phantoms illuminating themselves with the screen appeared almost simultaneously, one of them being recognised by a participant as his brother who was killed in the Bolshevik war in 1920.

This was followed by a period of strong and beautiful light phenomena. Flames with a large nucleus of light and small nebulae were followed by groups of smaller lights which would suddenly concentrate into one larger light and then disperse again. One had the impression that these lights were attached to the fingertips of a human hand which created these beautiful effects by quickly moving its fingers. Predominantly these lights emitted strongly phosphorescent, green-yellow vapours, which spread an intense smell of ozone as they rapidly dispersed throughout the room.

After these phenomena disappeared, quite loud noises were heard close to the medium and in other areas of the room. At that point the medium again started to tremble violently and to groan. The participants reacted by collective deep breathing which calmed the medium.

The rustles then moved to the middle of the room and began, very discreetly, to repeat the same noises, as if rubbing hands on woven fabric. The impression was that there was a desire to draw the participants' attention in that direction. After a moment, at a distance of about a metre from the participants, two lights appeared suddenly and simultaneously. They were stronger and bigger than anything else seen at that séance. These lights, the size and shape of a human hand, emitted a great amount of luminous vapours, which together with the lights illuminated the middle of the room, thus illuminating the participants closest to it and the phantom itself. This turned out to be the figure of an elderly man of typically Eastern appearance, in a white sumptuous cloak which covered the head and seemed to flow through the arms bare to the elbows. The figure had a long but very thin beard, chestnut in colour, falling onto the chest in two thin curly strands. A thin moustache separated under the nose, forming a straight angle on the cheeks, and curled itself into the beard which gave the impression of being carefully groomed. The face was swarthy and ascetic, eyes dark, penetrating, set under thick and strongly drawn eyebrows. When the lights appeared in the room it became so bright that the figure could be examined in great detail, much better than when lit by even the most light-saturated screen.

This figure, moving forward, both hands with fingers pointing upwards, began to emit from them an enormous amount of phosphorescent vapour. It would bring its hands together, rub them, lift them up and stretch them forward. The participants, amazed by the clarity and richness of the phenomenon, were quiet, observing in silence the appearance of this increasingly clear figure in a cloud of luminous vapours. It is difficult to estimate the length of time during which the phenomenon was visible to the participants but it seemed to last longer than the earlier phantoms. After a moment the phantom brought its hands together, which caused the light emanations to dim so much that the figure itself suddenly became invisible, except for a moving group of lights, no longer similar in shape to luminous human hands. These lights then moved behind the participant closest to the medium. They spread into two foci and the same figure appeared again in full. Luminous vapours again began to rise to the ceiling. This second appearance lasted significantly longer than the first one in the middle of the room, and the phantom behaved similarly, except for the fact that it was making many more complicated movements with its hands, something like a blessing or what looked like luminous geometric figures created with quick diagonal hand movements.

The figure then disappeared without any sound, leaving the room full of phosphorescent mists and a strange smell, not like the smell of ozone mentioned earlier.

This was followed by a further display of lights, the scent of almond blossom, another apparition illuminated by its own light, and further phantoms illuminated by the screen (one of them responding to the request to rise above the table by appearing in that location as a torso), as well as a fleeting visit of a small animal.

After the séance, when the participants entered another room, Okołowicz noted that the female participant was wearing a Venetian necklace kept by the medium in the bureau. That necklace must have been taken out of the bureau during the séance and placed around her neck.

8. Summary of a report by Wojciech Stpiczyński[9] of the séance held on 21 June 1923. The author confesses to knowing nothing about spiritualism, but he had visited a dozen or so mediums during the previous 10 years without reaching any conclusions. He visited Kluski's séances twice, both times at Kluski's home, and this report is from the second séance. As far as possible, the author attempts to

---

[9] Wojciech Stpiczyński (1896-1936) - politician, writer and editor, one of the most radical followers of Józef Piłsudski. He took active part in the struggle for independence.

deal only with the facts, and he is aware of the limits of human powers of observation:

The room is an ordinary study, with desks, some books, a few pictures, and tasteful ornaments. The only thing out of the ordinary is the presence on a small oval table of a luminous screen. Colonel Okołowicz, the host's closest friend, checks the participants. They then shut themselves off from the rest of the apartment by locking the door and drawing the curtain. The séance is nearly abandoned, because the host (the medium) is exhausted, but he decides to continue.

It is 23:00 hours; the medium sits on a hard chair with General Mariusz Zaruski on his right, then Lieutenant Modrzejewski on his right, then, going around the table, Janina Czuprykowska, Zygmunt Mostowski, Colonel Okołowicz and the author, six persons altogether.

The Colonel extinguishes the light, observing the usual procedure (the red light is turned on, a hand chain is formed, people maintain a relaxed, low conversation and breathe regularly). The medium falls into a trance, and the red light goes out at the same time.

Darkness, eyes adjust. Someone spots a little light under the ceiling, red, swinging, like a tiny electric lamp, circling, arching, spiralling, moving extremely fast or very slowly; then another, then another, a whole gamut of these will-of-the-wisps which appear and disappear all over the place, under the ceiling and at eye level. Participants are exclaiming, then go quiet as they begin to hear something that sounds like the rubbing of soft, silky material against the edges of the furniture, then the clearly audible sound of the wooden box on the desk at the other end of the room being opened and shut, a rustling, as if of papers being moved, and then silence. Then Mostowski declares that he has been touched, and so has the Colonel, who begins a kind of dialogue with this "someone" whose presence we hear, and some of us feel, but our "guest" says nothing. He does, however, react to wishes, is willing and gentle, says nothing, but understands everything. He does not demonstrate any will of his own but surrenders to that of others. The participants are trying to see him. There is excitement and uncertainty, straining attention. The medium can be heard and felt, he is trembling and his breathing is uneven. The door is locked from the inside, nobody could have got in but "someone" is there ... and then silence.

Before they have a chance to feel disappointed, a new phenomenon draws their attention. A sudden flash of lights high under the ceiling, a light shield, like a small moon with a cold light, is orbiting a regular circle with the radius of 1.5 – 2 metres. It is moving fast, and suddenly its motion changes from horizontal on high to vertical. The shield drops to eye level and then up again, a number of times. This allows the participants to work out what is happening, at least in part. It is the luminescent screen, which until then had been lying on the table and which had been lifted by an invisible hand and used to create the phenomenon.

[The author thinks these were signals intended for them, because as soon as they realised what was happening, the screen dropped onto the table for a moment, only to move along it and be raised to eye level. It hangs there momentarily, producing a streak of anaemic greenish light. The author, who counts himself among sceptics, cannot find a normal explanation. A non-believer, he begins to consider the possibility of spirits.]

An outline of a head appears in the greenish light of the screen. It emerges from darkness and slowly approaches the luminous screen, becoming increasingly real and more alive. The participants exchange observations, they see ginger facial hair, a wrinkled face, wide open eyes looking ahead under the brim of a cap, an irregular nose, and pale, sunken cheeks...

"but the picture is not complete. It has no plasticity, no depth, it is like an old portrait in the light of the moon."

"I cannot remember whether someone said it aloud, or whether the 'phantom' gained the information before it was uttered, but the screen held in 'its' hand started to move around its head in a circle lighting it from all sides. At a certain moment any doubts about its plasticity were removed."

The Colonel remarks that this is a Russian general. The author has no doubt that it is the uniform of a Russian officer, with details such as the cap with the officer's oval bow in the middle, and gold officer's stripes on the shoulders. The "General" approaches General Zaruski and lights himself for him. Looking closely at him, Zaruski recognises the phantom as Komarov and asks in Russian, "Is it you?", after which the phantom looks happier and salutes with its hand a number of times. The lips could clearly be seen to move, but there was no sound except for a kind of soundless whisper. This may have been caused by the participants becoming noisier due to the excitement. The phantom gave a military bow to his counterpart and for a moment approached each participant, including the author. The screen then returned to the table and the phantom disappeared. The author then asks:

> "But how, out of what elements, does human flesh, accurate, perfect, living, vibrant, form itself? What force reproduces with dazzling accuracy material objects, silk fabrics, rough baize of a military uniform, metal edging on military caps, the leather of shoes and gloves, all these things that the apparitions are wearing – and what happens to all these costumes when after a moment the phantom silently dissolves. [...] do they contradict their material existence or do they mock experimental science and the wisdom of this world?"

He then considers the possibility of hallucination or illusion. The participants take deep regular breaths, having become excited. Once they return to normal, another phantom appears, a young Polish officer, again in great detail, clearly familiar to the other participants. The Colonel exchanges greetings and shakes its hand, but the author only hears the Colonel's voice. The officer then approaches General Zaruski and seems to try to remind him of something, bowing and smiling.

The author then tries to reconcile his worldview (this world is all there is) with what he is seeing:

> Secure in my disbelief, assured of the reality of visual perceptions, I still see in greatest detail the young, laughing face of the phantom officer bending over my neighbour, the general, and I hear its presence confirmed by the participants.

After looking deeply into the phantom's face, whose features are at times difficult to make out because of the lighting, the General says that this is Lieutenant Topór-Kisielnicki, to which the Colonel replies that yes, it is, and that he thought he knew him but could not remember the name. Being recognised makes the phantom enthusiastic, it grabs and shakes the General's hand, moving its face even closer, trying to light it, followed by the characteristic sound of clicking heels and jangling spurs as the officer gives a military bow.

> After a moment the illuminated face was before me, I felt a strong clasp on my left forearm with a man's hand and an energetic kiss on my forehead. It seemed to me like a response to my doubts and scepticism – even today, whenever I think of that moment, I feel the

touch of warm lips and the resistance of teeth against the hard surface of my forehead, so characteristic of that type of energetic kiss on earth.

A number of phantoms followed, very much like the ones described, and none which the author recognised, which enabled him to observe the process for its own sake, with the influence of suggestion (if such were involved) very much reduced.

There was one more phenomenon that was most affective, the light phenomenon involving the appearance of the "Assyrian priest", as he was described by Colonel Okołowicz. The phantom looked like a beautiful old man, reminiscent of the inspired Rabindranat Tagore, in a flowing white robe, and it illuminated itself with its own pale green light.

... at a silent moment, when after the departure of the extraordinary guests we were trying to order our thoughts and rest our tired eyes in undisturbed darkness, supporting this process with deep breathing in order to help the medium, suddenly, just above the table, there appeared an initially weak, etheric swirl of light. At first it resembled phosphorescent smoke, swirling and energetically swaying in an invisible, transparent, and non-existent vessel. It then slowly began to lose its initial shape, as if it was pouring out onto a flat but uneven surface. At the same time the intensity of the phenomenon grew very quickly, finally revealing its origin (if one could describe it so). Thus, at the height of about 50 cm above the table, an irregular and mobile rag of intense light appeared, which spurted upwards a bright streak of light-green rays, in which a wave of air was clearly vibrating, mixed with the vapour: the kind of phenomenon you might see at night in a field sitting by a fire. A strong smell of ozone hit our nostrils. We observed it all together and were aware of its presence in the room afterwards." [...]

The vibrating, mobile, strange and shapeless rag of light, disturbing in its nervous agitation, suddenly started to rise in a slow movement, at the same time expanding its surface and stopping vertically at the height of 1.5 metre above the table. Its shape does not bring to mind anything of a similar kind; it is irregular and somewhat blurred in its contours with an intense phosphorescence, which flows down it in thick and seemingly misty streaks. But this luminous mass suspended in the air divides into two parts, which push away from each other in the horizontal plane, then descending and approaching each other, again in the horizontal plane, above the table. Having outlined a regular rectangle in space, they combine and return to their original state. After a moment the motion increases, is repeated, then there is another division, separation and descent, this time clearly along the lines of a triangle. This phenomenon is repeated a number of times. At one point we discover something staggering; the shining mass is two human hands. Although their shape is not sharp because of the strong phosphorescence, we can distinguish quite clearly shining hands and fingers, which at times open wide and are thus easy to recognise. In the rays of the phosphorescent hands we finally see the head of their owner: an outline of a charming grey-haired old man with a youthful face, splendid in the dignity of his beard and the silkiness of his snow-white robes, the "Assyrian archpriest".

As the numbers of apparitions increased, the medium trembled more frequently, and this trembling eventually resembled nervous attacks, which meant that it was necessary to stop the séance (in the usual manner). The séance lasted one hour and three quarters. Kluski rested, and when he came to he remembered nothing. They talked for a long time, listening with great interest to the stories related by Kluski's wife about the episodes from his life which indicated his strange mediumistic powers and nervous condition.

Late at night I shake the hand of this amazing man, in whom there seems to be nothing fascinating, nothing unusual or hypnotic – perhaps only his great gentleness and kindness towards all around him. We have not seen each other since that time.

9. The report by Prosper Szmurło, an experienced psychic researcher, relates to the séance which took place on 30 January 1924 at Kluski's apartment in Warsaw. It was published in *Zagadnienia Metapsychiczne* in 1925, and is given here in full in view of the amount of detail it contains.

Location of the séance

The séance took place in a long narrow room, approximately 3 x 6 metres, on the fourth floor, with one window looking out onto the street, with the curtain drawn, and with two doors. One door, opposite the window, leads to a corridor outside the apartment. It is firmly locked with a key and a chain, partially blocked with furniture and has a curtain across it[10]. The other door is small, in the side wall, with a glass pane at the top, and leads to the hall. It is separated from the first door by a fireplace with a mirror above it. On the mantelpiece there is a clock with a shining face and a red electric lamp (with a glass lampshade). Between the fireplace and the wall, next to the curtain covering the door, there is a small oval table around which are placed 7 chairs. The furniture consists of a desk under the window with a typewriter on it, a settee placed against the wall, chairs, and a dresser containing a statuette representing the column of King Sigismund together with other ornamental objects in it. On the walls there are pictures, miniatures, a knife, an antique sword, a carved cane, etc.

Conditions of the séance and the participants

The séance begins at 10.20 pm. The red electric lamp on the mantelpiece is on. Those present, seven in total, take their places around the table in the corner of the room, in the following order, according to the instructions of the séance leader, Colonel Okołowicz: 1. the medium, Franek Kluski at the narrower end of the table facing the door to the hall with his back to the wall; 2. on his left Lieutenant Modrzejewski [Kluski's son]; 3. General Edward Szpakowski[11]; 4. Prosper Szmurło; 5. facing the medium with his back to the door to the hall is Colonel Norbert Okołowicz (participants 3, 4 and 5 are all members of the Warsaw Psychophysical Society); 6. Lieutenant Siemieński and 7.

---

[10] The presence of this door, which might be regarded as a possible way for accomplices to enter, was not a secret, neither was its unused state. It should also be mentioned that Okołowicz summarises a set of six séances which took place in his own apartment, conducted in the presence of the same 6-8 people and under the same conditions, which is why he treats them as one unit. They took place in a much smaller room, with the furniture arranged in such a way that after the medium and the participants sat down there was very little free space between the furniture and the sitters. The medium would sit with the furniture immediately behind his back, the table in front, and controllers at his sides. The other participants also sat in such a way that it was not possible to move around them without moving their chairs. This lack of space did not seem to influence the phenomena.

[11] Edward Szpakowski (1880-1942), lawyer and colonel in the Russian Imperial Army, general in the Polish army.

Mr Kowalski, Director of the Opera House, on the right hand of the medium. Lieutenant Modrzejewski, General Szpakowski and Prosper Szmurło have their backs to the window, and Lieutenant Siemieński and Mr Kowalski have their backs to the curtain drawn across the door to the outside corridor. This seating arrangement remains unchanged until the end of the séance. Three of the participants are taking part in a séance with this medium for the first time. All the participants, including the medium, hold hands, creating a chain which remains unbroken even for one moment. They describe their impressions as they occur. All of them, at the request of Colonel Okołowicz, at intervals breathe deeply and as rhythmically as possible. Those next to the medium say that he is falling into a trance almost immediately.

Light phenomena

After about a minute from the start of the séance Mr. Kowalski perceives a small light and, shortly afterwards, the light is observed by everyone else. From that moment until the end of the séance the lights appear almost constantly and die out. This is most intense at the beginning and at the end of the séance, perhaps somewhat less so during materialisations. This, however, may be due to the fact that all the attention is then concentrated on the apparitions and not on the lights. The little lights are of the size and shape of a hazelnut, blue in colour, as if electric, resembling the glow of glow-worms. They appear at the level of the heads of those present, often much higher and simultaneously at various points distant from each other. They whirl as if dancing in the air, travel along diverse curves and zig-zag lines and sometimes there is something that looks like a whole constellation of 3 to 6 lights close together, continuously moving and vibrating. Some leave behind a nebulous trace, some seem like little comets with tails or miniature spotlights throwing a narrow beam of light, 25-30 cm in length. There are nebulae or little clouds, poorly lit but still clearly visible to everyone in spite of the darkness. This happens mostly near the medium, above his head. Apart from the nebulae, there are sparks and balls of light constantly running in different directions, which gives the impression that something is being created, materialised there.

Odours

Soon after the appearance of the lights one can smell a scent which is difficult to describe. It resembles ozone, and then roses, sometimes detected during materialisations when an apparition moves closer.

Spontaneous switching off and lighting of the lamp

After about 8-10 minutes from the beginning of the séance, the electric lamp which stands on the mantelpiece and had not been touched, spontaneously turned itself off and then turned itself on just before the end of the séance, when the medium was awakening from his trance.

Sound phenomena

Immediately after the appearance of the light we heard a crack from the direction of the desk which stood at some distance under the window, and throughout the séance various noises, close to or further away from the medium, could be heard. They came, judging by the sound, from about six steps away. The noises sounded as if they were caused by sliding and moving objects such as furniture, glass, and china. Then footsteps could be heard clearly, as well as the breathing of the approaching apparitions. There was knocking while attempting to communicate with the apparitions by reciting the alphabet and, lastly, on a number of occasions there was loud hand clapping, like applause at the level of a person standing with his hands raised up. (To be described in more detail later).

Levitation and telekinesis

General Szpakowski remarked that the shining face of the clock on the mantelpiece would be visible for a moment and then disappear, which could be explained by one of the participants moving his head and sometimes obscuring the clock. The participants asked for the clock face to be covered by the apparition with its hand. After a moment we saw the clock being lifted up. It flew in a curved line in the air, and disappeared behind the backs of those sitting next to the curtain. At the same time we heard it being wound by some invisible hand.

Touches

A few minutes after the beginning of the séance, Mr Kowalski, sitting to the right of the medium, announced that he felt touches on his shoulders and his head, and felt some kind of fabric being spread there. Next, the others also became aware of being touched (General Szpakowski and myself, Prosper Szmurło). I was touched by two small, delicate, soft cool hands simultaneously on my forehead, then under my chin, on my ears and my shoulders, as if the person touching me was standing behind my back. The touches also took place a number of times afterwards and during materialisations.

Materialisations

1. After the phenomena described above, and ten or more minutes from the beginning of the séance, the round wooden screen 30 cm in diameter, with a handle, one side of which is coated with luminous paint, which was lying on the séance table, was lifted up towards the medium, and there, at the level approximately of a standing person, it lit a shape which then approached those present and leaned towards them. At the same time one could hear footsteps, rustles, sometimes even breathing, and altogether one had an awareness of some presence. When the shape approached General Szpakowski on his right side, I leant a little and saw in detail, in the light of the screen from the side, the face of a man with a black trimmed moustache and pursed lips, corners down, in a Polish military cap with a peak. I could also see the collar, part of the uniform, and the shoulders. The apparition saluted a number of times. Leaning further, I could see its profile clearly displayed against the screen, as well as the fingers and the sleeve of the saluting hand. The apparition then moved towards me and I saw its face even more clearly, quite close, at a distance of 15-20 cm, with all the details. The apparition then showed itself to Colonel Okołowicz, which allowed me to observe it a little from the side and the back, mainly the cheek. The face of the apparition was not flat, but gave the impression of a human face, made of flesh, of normal size. I observed the other apparitions in the same manner; i.e., not only when they approached me directly but also when they were next to my neighbours on the right and the left, i.e., General Szpakowski and Colonel Okołowicz. Some apparitions moved immediately towards

the participants who were sitting on the other side of the table without going around the table, but crossing it as if it did not exist or did not constitute an obstacle for them. The same applies to the fact that although we were sitting at the table very close together, touching each other's legs and shoulders (at least myself and General Szpakowski), some apparitions presented themselves between us in such a way as if they had no lower body, or as if that body interpenetrated our legs.

2. Immediately after the first apparition, we got a phantom lighting itself with the screen, as was the case with all the apparitions during this séance. The phantom leant towards Mr Kowalski, who sat next to the medium. Mr Kowalski looked at the apparition for a moment and recognised a young man who had been killed in the last war and whom, he said, he loved as his own son. Mr Kowalski said in a voice full of emotion: "Tadek, it's you!" The apparition nodded its head. Mr Kowalski asked it a number of questions and received answers, either by the nodding of the head or by triple knocking, or touching, which was supposed to be confirmation. After a moment Mr. Kowalski said that the apparition was kissing his hand.

3. During the séance Mr Kowalski was the only one to be approached by two other apparitions, which he said he recognised, particularly when their names or surnames were mentioned by using knocks or the alphabet spoken aloud. The first of them referred to itself as "Froniek".

4. The second apparition which, according to Mr. Kowalski, was of an elderly man with a big moustache, referred to itself (using the alphabet) as Mosdorf and, using the same means of communication, made up the phrase "You have wine". Mr Kowalski said that he often used to drink wine with the deceased. He did not continue with the alphabet although I think he might have received a longer response.

5. Everyone in turn was approached by the apparition of a woman with a white shawl over her head, and we smelled a strong scent of roses. The phantom touched General Szpakowski on his forehead. When it was next to me on my left I could clearly see its forehead, dark eyebrows, eyes, cheeks and straight nose. The lower part of the face was veiled. Suddenly it raised its hand and moved the veil away, showing its lips and chin. I examined it closely, but did not recognise it. The apparition made the sign of the cross on my forehead and turned to Colonel

Okołowicz and, against the screen, I watched the shape of her head and the folds of the veil, which looked as if it was made of a very delicate fabric. I moved my head and in fact I did touch something very light, like tulle. The same apparition illuminated a lock of its blonde hair for Mr. Kowalski, and then, holding the screen horizontally above the table, showed its hand. When asked it answered, using the alphabet, that its name was "Ala". Those who attended previous séances with this medium say that it had appeared before.

6. Almost immediately after, perhaps a few seconds, those closest to the medium saw a new apparition, an elderly man with a beard and a moustache, wearing a Russian military cap. The apparition approached General Szpakowski and saluted him more than a dozen times, lighting itself as usual with the screen, showing a man's face with a large beard divided into two parts, and then, twice, using the screen it displayed its epaulettes. General Szpakowski said that there was something familiar about it, but he could not remember the person. One of the participants suggested that this might be General Komarov, who had appeared previously. We could hear a number of knocks, which indicated that the apparition wanted to speak. Using the alphabet we learnt that its name was not Komarov but Makarov, whom General Szpakowski knew personally, while I only knew him from photographs and from his statue. General Szpakowski recalled that the apparition did resemble the late Admiral Makarov, but he could not make out clearly the markings on the epaulettes, just that they belonged to a general. When he mentioned the resemblance to Makarov, the apparition shook his hand three times. At the suggestion of those present, Szpakowski went on to ask the alleged Admiral Makarov whether he spoke Russian, to which the apparition responded by nodding its head. While the phantom was moving towards me, General Szpakowski firmly leant backwards and encountered resistance as of someone's body. When the apparition approached me I saw what I have already described but, in addition, I could also see the upper part of the uniform, a number of buttons, and something like the ribbon of a medal.

7. I felt quite a firm touch on my forehead as if of a warm hand, then on my nose, and invisible fingers removed my pince-nez. Next, a young female face with a veil bent over me. I looked closely for a few seconds. It seemed familiar, like Alina K. who had died 20 years previously, but I am not certain. I had the same impression about the first female

apparition and I even expected that, when the alphabet was used, the name would be Alina and not Ala. The first apparition seemed to me to be a little older and to have a longer nose. In my mind I ask the question whether the apparition knew me, asking it to answer by touching my shoulder and, at that very moment, I feel three light taps on my left shoulder. The apparition disappeared and, it seems, did not approach anyone else. My pince-nez was replaced on my nose again.

8. No apparitions are visible. The lights begin again to circle violently above the table. The leader of the séance, Colonel Okołowicz, thinks that the séance is coming to an end and suggests that all those present should concentrate on making the red electric lamp on the mantelpiece light up again, but this does not happen. After a few minutes the screen, on which General Szpakowski was resting his hand in error, is pulled away, lifted, and used to light an apparition in which some participants recognise the Italian soldier Battisti, familiar from earlier séances. When he stands next to me I see the face of a man aged about 30, in a cap, with a black moustache and a pointed beard, which becomes more apparent when his profile is visible against the screen. Mr Kowalski asks a number of questions in Italian, including, "Are you happy with Mussolini?", to which he receives a positive response of three knocks. When the screen is put back on the table, which means that the apparition is no longer visible, Colonel Okołowicz suggests that we should all say out loud, "Evviva Italia", which we do, and at the same time we hear strong applause high above our heads as an indication of Battisti's pleasure.

The little lights dance in the air, the medium is breathing heavily, and all those present try to bring him relief by breathing deeply and rhythmically. Finally the medium awakes and in a weak voice asks for water. Colonel Okołowicz immediately goes out to fetch it. Some of those present also leave the room and, after a moment, the electric (red) lamp lights itself spontaneously and the séance ends at 11.25 pm, that is, after one hour and five minutes. The medium, exhausted, recovers fully after a few minutes and takes part in the general conversation. Neither the medium's pulse nor weight were recorded before or after the séance.

General Szpakowski says that in his opinion all the apparitions shared some features, and seemed to resemble the medium. I personally also noticed some slight resemblance between the apparitions, particularly when one looked at them en face, although in profile they seemed to me to differ more, but even then they were not totally different types. I would also like to mention that they all gave me the impression of being human, flesh faces, but totally immobile ones, with a frozen expression, without any movement of eyes or mouth, or any mobility which I would be able to discern.

This report was written by myself, P. Szmurło, the day after the séance, on the basis of notes taken immediately after the séance.

Warsaw, 31 January 1924.
P. Szmurło, Edward Szpakowski
Additional comments by Norbert Okołowicz:

The report written by Mr Szmurło covers, in my opinion, almost in full the description of the phenomena also observed by myself. However, I would like to add a number of comments, supplementary items and observations which I could not communicate to Mr. Szmurło, not having seen him since the séance.

Thus, when describing the "location of the séance" it was not mentioned that the door to the room was locked with a key (twice), and that the key was left in the keyhole. There is no glass pane in that door (as reported by Mr Szmurło), but there is a mirror which on the side of the hall is held in place by a thick wooden board.

As to the "materialisation" in point 5, I must note that a different apparition approached myself and Mr. Szmurło, making a sign of the cross on his forehead, from the one which showed its hand against the screen to Mr Kowalski and which knocked to indicate the name "Ala". The first apparition was that of an elderly woman with grey hair and black eyes, the second of a young woman with thick blonde locks of hair. I saw the apparition of the elderly woman at nearly every séance starting with 25 December 1923, while the apparition calling itself "Ala" appeared at this séance only for the third time.

The apparition described in point 6 of "Materialisations", claiming to be Admiral Makarov, has been appearing at Kluski's séances for some time. It appeared for the first time in March 1921, then at the séances on

20 June 1921, 26 March 1922, 17 August 1923 and 24 May 1923. It would wear either an admiral's hat or an ordinary Russian officer's cap, but would always be in a uniform with a general's or admiral's epaulettes. It would always try to show off its epaulettes, lighting them as carefully as possible with the screen. The participants at those séances, however, were unable to describe these insignia precisely beyond stating that they were Russian. The inability to recognise these insignia seemed to upset the apparition.

The exceptionally difficult awakening of the medium was probably caused by the fact that the medium's neighbour, Mr Kowalski, wanted to hold on to the apparitions of those close to him for as long as possible, while the other neighbour, Lieutenant Modrzejewski, was determined to make the red light come on before the medium woke up. This caused the divergence between the participants' desires, so harmful during séances.

Warsaw, 23 February 1924.
Norbert Okołowicz

10. Excerpts from the description of the séance on 17 February 1924 by Boy-Żeleński (writer and journalist), published on 21 February 1924 in the newspaper "Kurjer Poranny"; they convey some of the light-hearted atmosphere which often prevailed when the sitters were at ease with each other:

… Let us move on to what I saw with my own eyes. I am by nature fairly critical, an ex-doctor and I have not the slightest doubt as to the reality of what I saw. […]

… the other participants start to arrive. Altogether there are seven of us, all men, three of us doctors (including myself), and two naturalists. All of them apart from me have been to these séances before.

Paraffin wax is melted in the hope of obtaining these famous moulds, one of the strangest phenomena which take place at the Kluski séances.

We take off our jackets and put newspapers on our knees, since, as old hands warn, paraffin can splash. In the midst of it all the electric lights start going off. Old hands do not attach importance to it, explaining that this often happens before a séance [...] At our editorial office this would happen in Kluski's presence without a séance.

The light is turned off and only a little red lamp is left on. On the table there is a round luminous screen. In the middle of the table there is a tub with warm paraffin wax. [...]

... all those present must keep their hands on the table, touching lightly with the little fingers. It is alright to talk, there is absolutely no requirement for a lofty atmosphere - on the contrary, the mood is thoroughly rational and light-hearted.

The first phenomenon appears after a few minutes: lights in the air. Soon the electric red lamp goes out by itself. The lights become more numerous, they swing low over the table, and produce a light mist. There is a characteristic ozone smell in the air.

One of those present says that he feels a touch. Soon I also feel a touch on my shoulder. In a moment warm fingers touch mine. I want to hold on to them but lightly they slip out. I feel that there is a trace of wax left on my fingers. There is something lying in front of me on the table, also in front of one of the others. They tell me that it is a paraffin mould of the apparition's hand.

In the meantime a luminous disc rises and lightly swings in the air, like a small moon. It rises up to the ceiling, and then it circles above our heads. Somebody says that he can see an apparition and that he recognises it. The apparition is an army lieutenant who had already appeared at other séances. In a moment the light disc floats towards me across the air, illuminating clearly a man's head in a military cap. I can see the head quite three-dimensionally, it moves, I can see it en face and then in profile. The disc is at an angle to it, clearly as if to illuminate it. They tell me to ask the apparition to do something, I ask it, "Stroke my hair". It strokes. "Kiss me." It kisses. I feel a real kiss on my face. I get the impression that there is a faint smell of alcohol in the air. I say, "Seems as if the lieutenant whiffs of vodka a little." A number of knocks are heard, which means that the apparition wants to speak. The séance leader pronounces letters, the apparition points to them by knocking. It knocks, "Thaddeus reeks of vodka." Its hand lightly takes my head and bends me towards my neighbour, at the same time bending his head towards mine. My neighbour's first name is Thaddeus, he is a well known doctor and an experienced psychic investigator. He laughs and says, "True, it's me. I had a couple of glasses of vodka with my dinner". Clearly, the apparition felt offended by the unjust accusation.

The apparition disappears, another one arrives. Those present recognise this one as well. It is an Italian, Battisti. Battisti appeared to Kluski for the first time in Italy a few months ago, and was recognised by the Italians present at the séance. He is a popular hero of the last war, hanged by the Austrians for running away from them to the Italian army. I know a little Italian, so I improvise a frivolous Italian couplet. The response is loud clapping and a low voice saying, "Bravo!" The apparition bends over my neighbour, and the insignia of an Italian army private are visible on its collar. I speak to it. It comes over to me and does little errands.

The participants talk to Battisti, explaining to me his appearances at the Kluski séances in Italy. Someone jokes, "So how did he get here? By train?" The response to this is a loud noise as of objects being broken, and the joker gets a thump on the back. The phantom disappears. I am told that apparitions do not like ironic or aggressive treatment. In themselves they tend to be polite and friendly.

As for my own feelings, strangely enough I do not fear these apparitions. The lieutenant gives me a weird feeling, but the Italian creates a really nice, friendly impression.

I forgot to mention that at one stage the tub with the paraffin noiselessly disappeared from the table. After the séance it was found under the settee, while on the table was found the pipe of one of the participants, which was originally left on another piece of furniture.

The phenomena weaken, the medium must be tired. One of those present says "scent of roses". The scent must be moving about. I can only smell it after a while, but it is very strong.

It is time to end the séance. "Turn on the light," says the séance leader, "we're finishing now." After a while the little red lamp comes on by itself. We break the circle and come out, taking our two moulds.

Somebody stays with Kluski.

I look with curiosity at the mould left by the apparition. It is a very thin and delicate mould of a hand up to the wrist; two fingers straight, two bent. It is as if somebody immersed his hand in paraffin and took it out with a thin layer on, but it is a physical impossibility to take a living hand out of such a mould.

[...]

The lady of the house and the lovely daughter-in-law offer us coffee and chocolates. They don't attend the séances themselves, they don't like it. My amazingly gifted friend comes back into the sitting room. It is painful to watch him: eyes unfocused, face swollen, he is coughing blood into his handkerchief (one of the doctors tells me it is not a serious haemorrhage, but momentary bleeding). Whoever saw him in that state would not entertain the thought that this man invited us here to dupe us.

[...]

11. Summary of a report of a séance held on 22 May 1924 in Italy, at a totally unfamiliar location, written by the Polish Consul in Milan.

I confirm that on 22 May 1924 I took part in a séance with the medium Franek Kluski in Milan, in a hotel room reserved by Mr. Giacomo Venturi, Director of Bank Commerciale Italiana. Apart from myself, the other participants were Mr Venturi, his wife, and his brother.

Those present sat as follows: Mr Giacomo Venturi controlled the left hand of the medium, I the right, and on my right sat Mme Venturi, and Mr Giovanni Venturi between her and Mr Giacomo Venturi."

The séance started at 23:00 hours and lasted about half an hour. It was in total darkness. There were greenish little lights, and a strong smell of ozone remained throughout. The lights approached the sitters, then the shadow of a human hand could be seen in the light of the luminous screen lying on the table. The author of the report felt the touch of a warm, as if a child's, hand on his face and hands, as did the others. Then a beautiful woman appeared, in a Renaissance costume, with long hair, very much like Beatrice d'Este whose portrait hung in the room. When director Giacomo Venturi commented that he could smell roses strongly, the author of the report said he could not. The phantom then approached him (the author) again and blew towards him, at which point he also smelt a strong scent of roses. Paraffin splashing followed, and they could hear two objects fall on the floor. Then, in spite of the darkness, they saw the paraffin wax container rise above their heads. This was followed by the phantom of a man in his 40s, with gingery facial hair, unknown to those present, and a phantom recognised by Giacomo Venturi as Cesare Battisti. It was lighting itself with a greenish light from its hands. It confirmed that it was Battisti and, on hearing that Venturi had been an Italian officer and fought together with Battisti, it hugged him. Clapping was heard below the ceiling when Battisti and Italy were cheered. (The author did not know what Battisti looked like, but recognised the photograph he saw two weeks later as being that of the phantom from the séance). The séance ended because of the medium's exhaustion. When the light was turned on two paraffin moulds were found on the table, a male hand, and a small one, like a child's. The paraffin wax container was on the floor in the neighbouring closet, the door to which had been open.

> I held the medium's right hand throughout the séance and I did not let it go even after the end of the séance. Apart from Mr Venturi all the participants were novices. The medium felt very weak and vomited afterwards. In my opinion, hypnosis, hallucination, etc., were impossible. Milan, 3 November 1924. Zdzisław Marski, Consul of the Republic of Poland in Milan.

12. Even though F.W. Pawłowski's account, published in the *Journal of the American Society for Psychical Research* in September 1925, does not provide a séance record, it does give a very clear report of things he had seen with his own eyes in the course of several séances.

These sittings took place in 1924.

After describing the conditions under which the séances normally took place, Pawłowski describes his own experiences:

> After a few strong and distinct raps in the table or in the walls, bright bluish stars appear and begin to move high above the table, near the

ceiling. (Rooms in Warsaw apartments are rather high, more than twelve feet). The stars range in size from that of a pea to that of a filbert, until there are about a dozen of them. They move all over the space above the sitters with considerable rapidity (up to about three or four feet per second) in all directions, forming clusters and pairs. Some of them disappear, some of them (the pairs) come down, approaching the sitters.

When they approached me to a distance of about 16 inches, I recognized to my great astonishment that they were human eyes looking at me. Within a few seconds such a pair of eyes develops into a complete human head, and with a hand having a luminous palm illuminating it clearly. The hand will move around the head as if to show itself more clearly to the onlooker, the eyes looking at one intensely and the face smiling most pleasantly.

I have seen a number of such heads, sometimes two at a time, moving through the air like drifting toy balloons from one sitter to another, and upon such a request as "please come to me" from a distant sitter, the head will most obligingly shoot toward him the shortest way (frequently across the table), at a considerable velocity, like the stars.

Pawłowski then divides his experiences into categories. Thus, he heard and felt the raps and had the impression that they came from within the table or wall rather than from the surface. His impressions of the apparitions includes the invisible ones whose presence manifests itself through the sounds of footsteps, the creaking floor, and the touch of the living hands, while the visible apparitions light themselves with the screen and can also be seen in the red light. In his own words:

The light from the plaque is so good that I could see the pores and down on the skin of their faces and hands. On the nose of an older man-apparition I could see clearly the complicated pattern made by the crooked, tiny red blood vessels; I could examine closely the texture of the material of their clothes. I examined a number of them at such close distance that I could hear their breathing and feel their breath upon my face.

On two occasions, Pawłowski also saw the highest type of apparition, both times the same subject, [...] a completely luminous one of an old man. The apparition makes an impression of a light column. The light from him was so strong that it illuminated all of the sitters and even the more distant objects in the room. His hands (palms) and the region of the heart were much more strongly luminous than the rest of the body.

He appeared in the middle of the room quite a distance from us. The table was in the corner of the room and the medium in the very corner. The visitant wore a high conical hat and a long gown hanging in deep folds. He proceeded toward us with majestic steps, his gown flowing, describing with his hands some large triangular figures, and speaking in a deep and solemn voice. He stood just behind my back for at least ten seconds, waving his fuming hands above us and talking all the time. Then he drew back to a distant part of the room and vanished. He produced such a large quantity of ozone that the room was full of it even long after the séance. He was a very old man with a long gray beard. His language was rather guttural, and incomprehensible to all of us (known to the regulars as Assyrian priest).

Pawłowski also comments on the light emitted by the apparition, confirming reports from other witnesses:

Many of the apparitions have luminous hands, i.e., the palms of their hands are luminous. The white, slightly greenish, light is so strong that when they move their hands about their heads and bodies I could examine them just as well as when the former type of apparitions used the luminous plaques. They illuminate themselves in this manner seemingly for the benefit of the sitters; also, they move their hands about the sitters, apparently to examine them on their part. On such occasions I could clearly see that the light was not perfectly steady, but, on the contrary, vibrated, changing in intensity in various places, although the general or overall intensity of the palm remained about the same. I could see also some more brilliant spots, like sparks, moving in zigzagging and diverging paths from the wrist toward the fingers. At the same time I smelled ozone streaming in rather large quantity from their palms.

As for animal apparitions, Pawłowski saw two of them, a squirrel and a dog, which "behaved in a perfectly natural way, the squirrel jumping on the table ... and the dog running about, wagging its tail, jumping on the laps and licking the faces of the sitters". He also experienced the presence of the "Pithecanthropus", a hairy creature resembling an ape which rubbed itself against him and gave out a peculiar smell, like that of a wet dog.

Phantoms in full light

Reports of these do not form part of "official" reports, since they were experienced outside the séances, usually only in the presence of the medium and his family or friends. Okołowicz witnessed them on a number of occasions, and describes a particular event when other witnesses were present. On 7 May 1920, at around 21:00, the medium and the visitors were sitting and talking in the light of two standard lamps about 5 m away from each other. The conversation had nothing to do with psychical research. Suddenly, one of those present noted that just by the (closed) door there appeared a white, thick cloud the height of a person. It was all the clearer because the lamp stood by the door lighting it very thoroughly. When the others started paying attention, the misty cloud moved towards the middle of the room and suddenly became a tall elderly man with a large dark beard, wearing a white burnus and a white head wrap. This made a big impression on those present, including the medium, who seemed fully conscious. The figure bowed in the Eastern manner, touching its forehead and chest and then stood motionless. Those present were so astounded that for a while there was silence. Finally, someone invited the phantom to sit down and it did so on the floor in the Eastern manner, with its legs tucked under it. A conversation was started, with the phantom answering in sign language and by knocking (the knocking came from a dark corner a few metres away), but without making any movements while the knocking took place. It claimed to be a Turk captured during a battle between the Polish army and Turks 250 years previously. It also claimed not to be able to speak because its tongue had been cut out by an ancestor of one of those present. It was noted that while at times the phantom seemed to be just like a living person, every so often it would become transparent and misty, with its contours blurring, and that its eyes and eye sockets seem to burn with a strange light. It was asked whether it wanted to smoke and, after it accepted the offer, it was suggested that it should get a cigarette from a box about two metres away from it, in the middle of the table. All those present admitted afterwards that they were a little nervous and this made them reluctant to move. The phantom, without moving from where it sat, stretched its hand towards the table, the hand becoming elongated and nebula-like. A moment later it became normal and it was holding the cigarettes, which it offered to those present. It then got up and lifted a sword, which was hanging on the wall, from its scabbard, using only one hand even though normally the sword did not come out of the scabbard easily. Standing in the middle of the room it made a few movements with the sword, as if to show it knew how to use it, then put it back in the scabbard, moved towards the door, changed into a misty cloud and disappeared. Those present immediately went out into the hallway but there was nothing to see. Everyone agreed that this phantom made an incomparably greater impression on them than the phantoms seen in the darkened séances.

On another occasion, the medium was ill and lying on the settee. Okołowicz and another visitor were talking, the room being light, with all of them able to see each other quite clearly. Suddenly from inside the bookcase (about 1m from the medium's head) there was a knocking. More knocks came from high above the bookcase and from the opposite corner, from the dresser about 3 m from them, low down near the floor. They become interested in the knocks from the bookcase and the other knocks died down. They went through the alphabet and a discussion took place in which the medium, who was smoking, also participated. The discussion became heated and the knocks clearer, with the Chinese vase on top of the bookcase bouncing up and down. They were told they would see a phantom. The knocking stopped and suddenly they saw, in a chair next to the desk (1m from the person sitting in the middle of the room), a misty figure, sitting immobile next to the desk. It resembled a fat monk in a pale habit, with its contours and face blurred. Okołowicz compared its appearance with that of the friend sitting opposite him, whom he could see clearly, with the light illuminating him on one side while the other was in shadow; however, in the case of the phantom, both sides were equally bright-misty, as if transparent. They started a conversation with the phantom, who responded by knocking with a wooden holder on a brass ashtray. The medium was fully conscious and participating in the conversation.

Séance to observe interaction with the lighting

Okołowicz does not provide the exact date, but says that after a successful séance in April 1920 he and another participant, JD, decided to hold another short sitting. The red lamp was dimmed, the white light turned off, and Kluski sat down in the corner squeezed between Okołowicz and JD, and blocked in by the table. His hands were resting on the table, not held by either of his neighbours. After a moment, when the medium was entranced and they started hearing rustlings, JD said, turning towards the medium, "turn off the light". To their surprise, the medium got up and extricating himself with difficulty from his seat went, like a somnambulist, to the lamp, reached out with his hand, on which they suddenly saw highly phosphorescent lights, and turned off the light using the switch, after which he returned to his seat.

After a moment and a whispered discussion, they decided to repeat the experiment but using direct hand control. They turned the red light on again and, having grasped the medium's hands, they said, "turn off the light". While Okołowicz looked at the light, JD looked at the medium. Immediately afterwards the medium made a movement as if trying to get up, and they saw a third hand which seemed to grow out of his right shoulder and quickly reach towards the lamp. From the fingers to the elbow it looked like a real physical hand, but then it became a sort of misty streak which seemed to disappear close to the medium. The hand turned the light off quite visibly, as before, by turning off the switch. They decided to try again and, having re-lit the lamp and holding the medium's hands (he immediately became entranced), they said again, looking at the lamp, "let the lamp go out". A few seconds later the lamp was turned off, but the medium did not move at all and there was nothing at all anywhere near the lamp.

Séances to observe the materialisation process

In July 1919 Okołowicz started to try and observe the process of materialisation. With this aim, they would sit the medium on a chair in the middle of the room. Okołowicz would sit on the medium's left, close up against his chair, and the person on Kluski's other side would do the same. Each would hold Kluski's hand with one hand, and in the other hand would hold a small screen which constantly illuminated the medium on each side and on the back. They also immobilised the medium's knees with their own. Also, on Okołowicz's left side stood a large phosphorescent screen (80 x 100cm) which lit an area about 2 m^2 in front of the medium and the controllers with a stream of light from almost the floor level up to 120 cm and over 100 cm wide. Across from this second screen sat another person whose task it was to observe everything which could be seen against the screen. They thus formed a three-sided rectangle, with the medium and the controllers on one side, the screen on their left, and the observers on the right. Opposite the medium, beyond the light, stood the furniture, and behind the medium and the controllers, some 2 metres away, stood a red light.

The controls meant that the medium could not make any move, and no phenomenon could take place without being observed. The medium was mostly conscious, sometimes falling into a short trance. After the white light was turned off, they would start manipulating the screens in order to keep the medium constantly illuminated. After a few minutes during which the medium entered trance state, they would start hearing rustlings and knocks from the dark areas of the room, and see small lights. On one occasion, when the medium breathed deeply, Okołowicz saw suddenly that a bushy head of hair had formed on Kluski's head at the same time, and under his lower jaw there appeared a long beard, while his whole body seemed shrouded in mist. This lasted a moment, and then a kind of greyish mist separated from the medium and, still in a human shape, floated through the light from the big screen and disappeared in a dark place by the window, as if into the floor. Immediately after this the medium became conscious, while under the window could be heard knocks, rustles, and the lip-smacking usually produced by the "primitive man". The experiment involving these controls was repeated during the following séances with similar results and, to those observing the large screen, it seemed as if a misty, transparent body resembling a human shape was for a moment visible against the screen.

Okołowicz thought that they had observed the process of materialisation, but a few days later, under exactly the same conditions, phantoms of human shapes, including the "primitive man", appeared in dark places away from the medium even though nothing was observed forming on him. Further experiments also produced both kinds of result.

3.6. The Permanent Paranormal Object or The Moulds Controversy

Attempts to create a Permanent Paranormal Object through taking impressions of "ghostly" hands in the form of paraffin wax gloves date back to 1876, when William Denton first tried such a procedure. With Kluski, attempts to obtain wax moulds started from the earliest séances in 1919, and the people instrumental in introducing this idea were two Polish researchers, medical doctors J. Guirard and T. Sokołowski. The moulds would only very occasionally be similar to Kluski's hands but, in the early period, there was no attempt to submit these objects to special examination. On average, about 3 moulds would be produced in a séance but very few of them survived because of their fragility.

Much has been written about the formation of the 'Kluski hands'. Most of this writing offers explanations of how moulds of this kind could be produced at a séance by natural means, which is a good starting point for a discussion of what is possible and when. I summarise here the various descriptions offered, making use of a number of publications (Varvoglis 2002; Gaunt 2012; Polidoro & Garlaschelli 1997; Coleman 1994) regardless of whether they judge the Kluski phenomena to be fraudulent or genuine.

Moulds can be created by natural means in a number of ways. One involves a variety of methods for removing, or making smaller, the object after a wax mould of it has been created. These would include using a tourniquet around the arm to make the hand swell while the mould is being made, with the removal of the tourniquet making the hand smaller and therefore easier to slip out; using a prefabricated soluble cast which would disappear without a trace; or a prefabricated inflatable cast which could be withdrawn after deflation. Another method would be to use a rigid cast and various techniques for cutting the mould to remove it and then joining the parts once the cast has been removed, since hot paraffin has a degree of plasticity.

All these activities require equipment, time (taking great care with removing the fragile paraffin glove), and an amazing degree of dexterity (particularly when creating two clasped hands, hands with bent fingers, or feet, etc.), highly unlikely to be achieved in the dark. One can only assume that these explanations concern purely the possibility of producing such moulds in principle, since it would be absurd to expect these procedures to be adopted during séances. It would not have been possible for Kluski or an accomplice to free their hands, produce intricate moulds, and then wait for them to cool for 15 to 20 minutes, unless there was collusion amongst the participants at all the séances when moulds were produced, of which there were literally hundreds. While the natural explanations put forward so far have been based on the research conducted by Geley and Richet at the IMI in Paris (without actually accusing them of fraud which, however, is the logical conclusion of the argument), this accusation would have to be extended to almost all those who sat with Kluski.

If Kluski could not have produced the moulds fraudulently during the séance, the next most obvious scenario is that moulds of all shapes and sizes were prepared beforehand, and smuggled into the séance room by the medium and his accomplices. The problem with that explanation is what actually happened at so many séances: splashing of the wax would be heard (and sometimes felt), and within a minute or so warm, soft gloves, different in size, character, and arrangement, would drop on sitters's hands or in their laps, so thin (1mm) and fragile that most of them got damaged and did not survive. However, most of them did survive long enough for people to feel them when warm and soft, hang on to them, and examine them when cooled.

Some of the material in this chapter has not previously been reported outside Poland, but it is mainly supplementary to the experiments conducted in France by Gustave Geley, Charles Richet, and Count de Gramont at the IMI in Paris in 1920 which provide the best picture of how the moulds were obtained. Their aim was to obtain a Permanent Paranormal Object, and the controls which they employed have already been described elsewhere. The procedures adopted in the production of paraffin wax moulds are explained with great clarity by Mario Varvoglis (Varvoglis, 2002), and what follows are excerpts from his account:

> The sessions took place in low red light, which was sufficient to distinguish the outlines of those present. All sitters locked hands during the sessions. The experimenters were very much conscious of the hand-substitution trick, and were specifically vigilant about any such attempt. Typically, Kluski's hands (and not just the wrists) would be held by Dr. Geley on one side, and Charles Richet or Count de Gramont on the other. The experimenters also maintained permanent leg contact with the medium. All contacts were verified before the light was dimmed. Once the session had begun, the controllers would

give frequent reports, checking and verbally confirming their certitude that they are holding one of Kluski's hands.

The system used at the IMI involved a circular tank 30 centimeters in diameter, containing several kilograms of wax that floated on electrically heated water, thus producing a 10-cm deep layer of liquid wax. The system was placed on a table, in the center of the circle formed by the sitters, 60 centimeters in front of the medium. Rather than using a second bowl for cooling, the IMI researchers preferred to allow the wax moulds to rigidify on their own, this being, as we shall see, a precaution against fraud. Following the sessions, the investigators would pour plaster into the fragile wax moulds, to obtain a more permanent object ; once the plaster hardened, they would simply plunge the ensemble into boiling water and strip away the wax layer.

While the olfactory, visual and tactile phenomena came soon after sessions began, it generally took 15 to 20 minutes before any sign appeared that a mould was in the process of forming. The experimenters would first hear the sound of the 'hand' dipping into the paraffin, and then feel it touch their own hands, moist with warm wax. It would then be heard dipping in the container again, and finally come out and deposit itself next to them. Once begun, this whole process would evolve quite rapidly - within 1 to 2 minutes. As Geley remarked this was quite surprising, given that paraffin's normal time to solidify at room temperature is much longer.

December 27th session: Just prior to beginning, Richet and Geley had secretly added a bluish coloring agent to the paraffin. Control of the medium was considered excellent, with controllers regularly checking and verbally reporting 'I am holding the right hand', 'I am holding the left hand'. Splashing sounds were heard about twenty minutes into the session, and one to two minutes later two warm paraffin gloves were deposited next to the controllers. Both wax moulds had precisely the same bluish tint as that of the tank, strongly suggesting that these were indeed created during the séance, and not smuggled in by the medium. An additional control was the weighing of all substance. Prior to the experiment, the paraffin was 3.920 grams, while at the end of the session it weighed 3.800 grams. The two moulds weighed 50 grams, and there was considerable wax scattered near the medium (around 15 grams), on his clothing, and on the floor 3.5 meters away from him (about 25 grams). Insofar as the sum of these weights correspond very closely to the initial weight, this further establishes that the wax gloves were produced during the session. Finally, it should be mentioned that the wax moulds were less than a millimeter thick (thinner than a sheet of paper).

Further improvements were made in the next session, adding another substance, cholesterol, to the paraffin mix, demonstrating conclusively that the moulds were produced during the session. Also, one of the moulds produced was a child-sized foot and the other the lower part of an adult face. More séances were later held in Warsaw, with the participants finally observing luminous hands dipping into the paraffin. It is the Warsaw séances which we move on to now.

We have a very detailed report of the séance on 7 May 1921 (summarised here), held specifically for Dr Geley to obtain paraffin moulds at Kluski's apartment in Warsaw. This was a time of the medium's greatest weakness and passivity during a séance. Alongside the description of the sequence of the phenomena, we are also given a characterisation of the participants, their attitude to the medium and their moods, as well as some suppositions about their immediate influence on the shaping of the moulds.

Participants: Dr G. Geley, Dr J. Guirard, Ludomira Grzel., Zofja Okołowiczowa, Stanisław Jelski, Norbert Okołowicz.

Prior to the séance, all agreed to concentrate their wishes only on obtaining wax moulds. Everyone sat down, a hot paraffin container (60 cm long and 32 cm deep, oval, with a layer of about 5 cm of melted paraffin on a layer of hot water) was placed on the table. A luminous wooden screen (25 x 35 cm) was placed next to the container, shaped like a hand mirror, weighing about 300 g.

The séance lasted for over an hour, from 21:55 to 23:00. All participants maintained unbroken hand contact throughout, as did the controllers holding the medium's hands.

A few minutes after the main light was extinguished (with the red lamp on) it was noticed that the medium became entranced. Even before that, light phenomena appeared in the form of little stars, first singly, then a number of them together at a height of 0.5 to 1 m above the head of the medium and those next to him.

This was followed by rustling sounds next to the paraffin container and then those present heard the noise as if of a cold mould being gently placed on the table. The red lamp on the mantelpiece, about 2 m from the medium, went out at the same time.

The next phenomenon was the alternate splashing in the container and sounds of the table surface being in contact with dry paraffin moulds. Suddenly, in the opposite corner of the room, about 5 m from the medium, violent and uneven rustlings and noises could be heard, as if of blows with heavy objects hitting the side and top of the wardrobe and the table next to it. At the same time the controllers felt the medium's hands shake violently, as if in rhythm with these sounds, and his body was shaking as well.

After a moment, the screen which was lying next to the container rose about 1 m and fell down, shattering some of the moulds lying there. It attempted to rise a number of times but seemed to suddenly weaken and fall on the table or on the heads of the participants, who became anxious about these phenomena. One participant, wanting to stop further damage to the moulds, held on to the screen and pressed it with his knee to the table leg. However, the screen was pulled away by force and started travelling again, each trip ending like the first one. It was then carried beyond the table and for a moment was invisible.

During that time little lights appeared, like those which usually appeared at the beginning of a séance, and then, in a corner of the room, about 1.5 m from the medium, fast and irregular sounds began, even more violent than previously. Again, the medium had violent tremors in his hands and upper body, so strong that he was shaking the table and his neighbours. When the sounds and then the medium quietened down, the screen appeared again above the head of the medium's neighbour to his left and tried to illuminate a phantom which looked like a military man in a Polish uniform. This lasted briefly and tried to repeat itself a number of times but was very poorly visible because the screen kept dropping back as soon as it rose.

The screen then rose and showed briefly a blurry phantom bust in white. After this, it tried to illuminate the controllers and some other phantoms, unlike the two previous ones. These phenomena disappeared and new, weaker lights appeared, followed by the red lamp coming on, flickering, and finally staying on. The participants attempted to wake up the medium, who after a few minutes was sufficiently awake for a small white lamp, and then the ceiling light, to be turned on. This was the end of the séance.

After the ceiling light was turned on and the participants and the medium rose from the table, the side lamp kept turning itself on and off, while the red lamp stayed on continuously.

On the table were two moulds; one looked like a child's or a young woman's hand with the arm up to the elbow; the second one looked like a man's hand, also with the arm. The first one was partially broken in the middle by the falling screen and the second had the arm broken in a number of places. On the surface of the paraffin in the container two moulds were found, already partially dissolved; they looked like children's hands. The table, the hands, and the sleeves of some participants, as well as the floor near the table, were splashed with paraffin.

Okołowicz then provides a drawing (which, however, does not allow us to identify the numbered participants) and a description of the condition and attitude of the medium and of each participant in turn.

Medium – very exhausted physically and mentally, started the séance wanting to get the best possible moulds. In a heavy and turbulent trance throughout.

Participant 1 (controller) – almost always present, totally trusted by the medium and regarded as a positive factor, with a positive influence on the phenomena and the medium. The youngest of all there.

Participant 2 (controller) – regarded as quite a good factor, has taken part in séances more than a dozen times, liked by the medium. Focused throughout the séance on obtaining the best and greatest number of moulds. (It seems safe to assume that Dr Geley was participant No. 2 or No. 4, in view of these two being focused on obtaining wax moulds).

Participant 3 – liked by the medium, without any special desires regarding the phenomena. Had attended séances on more than a dozen occasions, in good condition physically and mentally.

Participant 4 – very much liked by the medium. Has his own established ideas about how moulds are formed. Very tired physically and mentally, exhausted by his professional commitments. Focused throughout the séance on obtaining moulds at the expense of other phenomena.

Participant 5 – frequent sitter, very positive, trusted by the medium. Against holding this séance and only wishing that it would not exhaust the medium and would come to an end. When that person sits next to the medium there is usually no trance, and the phenomena either do not happen or are very weak.

Participant 6 – very positive factor, totally trusted by the medium. For nearly two years almost always present at the séances, sometimes consciously influencing them. On that occasion, very tired physically and mentally. All this participant's desire was centred on supporting the medium's energies. No special wishes for the phenomena, just wanting a quiet séance.

Okołowicz then goes on to correlate, as far as possible, the participants' thoughts and feelings based on their accounts with the report of séance events and his own observations. Thus:

The general atmosphere at the beginning of the séance was calm. Okołowicz supposes that a human hand, together with the forearm, materialised at the bottom of the paraffin container and slowly emerged to the surface. This event was observed by participant No. 6[12]. After a moment the cooled mould is placed in front of participant No. 2. This is heard by everyone except the medium. The mould was probably placed there because of the desire of participant No. 2, supported by participant No. 4, but it could also have been simply that there was more space there.

After a moment those present hear a splash in the container and imagine that it was a materialised hand dipping into the paraffin to make a mould. As if to support this supposition, participant No. 1 is suddenly touched on the hand with a mould that is still hot. A voice saying, "I am touched on my hand by something like a hot mould," is heard. At this point participants 3 and 4 begin to wish fervently to be touched as well.

The finished mould goes back to the container, presumably to take an additional portion of paraffin onto its surface. Participants 1, 5, and 2 think, "better it does not touch anyone and produce a child's leg or hand". The finished mould, pushed back into the container by the desires of participants 3 and 4, cannot rise, because the desires of participants 1, 5, and 2 change its existing form. Finally the phenomenon ceases and the mould blends with the surface of the paraffin.

There is another splash, those present think, "a new mould is being formed", and in fact a mould can be seen rising above the table in the form of a nebulous smear, presumably being cooled. At that point participant No. 3 expresses aloud the opinion, "this is probably a child's

---

[12] Okołowicz also remarks that the moment of emergence was frequently observed on other occasions in the red light and the light of the screen, even though the moment of dipping of the materialised substance was not observed. However, more frequently a materialised hand could be seen dipping into the paraffin.

hand". Participant No. 4 first thinks, and then voices his contradiction, "No, this is definitely a child's leg." Participant No. 5 is thinking, "we have not had a mouth mould for such a long time." Then the phenomenon, not supported by sufficient focus of those present, loses power, falls down from a height, and breaks on the edge of the paraffin container.

This is followed by pleas, either voiced or mental, from the participants, "don't do this, don't destroy, make me a nice mould". In response to these requests, very different from the previous ones, the phenomena change, replaced by lights and knocks. The medium begins to move in an agitated manner, as if trying to intervene and fill the gap left by the participants' lack of focus. During that time participant No. 6 momentarily passes out.

The phenomena try to repeat themselves and the process of producing a mould, preceded by a splash, begins again. However, under the influence of participants 3 and 5 who want everything to happen close to them, the phenomenon is pulled towards the opposite end of the container where, no longer supported by attention, it is destroyed by falling onto the surface of the paraffin.

After a moment, the screen which is lying next to the finished moulds begins to move, as if trying to rise. Nearly all the participants, but particularly Nos. 2 and 4, become very anxious about preserving the existing moulds intact. The screen continues to flap nervously, as if unable to lift itself off the table. Participants Nos. 1 and 3 think, "what kind of phantom will light itself now?" The screen rises heavily and gives participant No. 6 the impression that it wants to shine on the finished moulds. Participants Nos. 2 and 4 think, "better make new moulds instead of waving the screen, or you'll destroy the finished ones". At that point the screen falls down and partially destroys the finished moulds.

The medium begins to move anxiously, and little lights appear intermittently as if trying to draw attention to themselves. All the participants become anxious. Noises can be heard, and participants Nos. 5 and 6 think, "let the red light come on and let's finish, the medium is so tired". Participant No. 2 wants at least one more mould and then to withdraw from the séance at once, to preserve the ones that are finished from destruction. Participant No. 4 imagines that the next mould will have a complicated finger arrangement, which will need a number of dippings in paraffin, and that this will last two minutes.

Participant No. 1 wants to see at least one more phantom before the red light comes on. Participant No. 3 has no special thoughts.

At that point the screen rises hesitantly and illuminates a figure; participant No. 2, worried about the finished moulds, tries to stop the development of this phenomenon with his thoughts, supported in this by participants Nos. 5 and 6. The screen falls down, damaging the moulds again.

Participants Nos. 1 and 5 wish aloud for the red light to come on and for the medium to wake up. Participants Nos. 4 and 3, and to some extent No. 2, want to see the phantom again. The screen rises quite quickly and illuminates the bust of a new phantom, which moves beyond the medium and shows itself to participant No. 2, as if looking for the best place where it can be supported by his interest and closeness to the medium.

Gradually the anxiety, excitement, and conflicting desires become difficult to control. Participants Nos. 6 and 5, supported by participant No. 1, want the séance to end. The red lamp flickers a number of times and then stays on, the medium wakes up and the hand chain is broken. White light is turned on but flickers, as if there was scattered "energy" around, still trying to fulfil the conflicting desires, or as if reflecting the nervous excitement of the participants.

Okołowicz also makes the general comment that after every séance in which moulds were attempted there were, apart from the perfectly formed ones, numerous traces of dripping on the table, on the participants' clothes, and on objects far from the medium. Apart from the drippings, there were always scraps of cold paraffin, as if traces of trials or parts of destroyed moulds, with traces of papillary lines.

This is a fascinating and rare attempt at gaining insight into the phenomena "from the inside", and it is a pity that no other attempts of this kind are recorded.

At a séance almost exactly a year later, on 5 May 1922, Geley witnessed the formation of the moulds and their relationship with the appearance of light, something confirmed by numerous statements by other witnesses on other occasions. His account is one of many quoted by Okołowicz:

> I am controlling the left hand of the medium. Present: St. Ossowiecki, Mme A.E., Lt. Col. Okołowicz, Dr Guirard, Mme Missiuro. The trance comes very quickly. Lights very varied and numerous appear close to the participants, sometimes very high, rise quickly and are of different sizes, of a pea or a nut. Sometimes they are multiple shining points, sometimes phosphorescent nebulae with a condensed centre.

At other times, there are groups of lights like a chandelier made up of 4-6 shining points. Every now and again a shining nebula can be seen on the head of the medium, which gives the impression of a shining vapour rising from the head. I am frequently touched by the light and I then feel the touch of hands or fingers. Suddenly we see two shining points which float at the height of 1.5-2 m above the paraffin container. When all attention is focused on them, the lights slowly descend and enter the container. We can hear the splashing of paraffin. The lights emerge from the container, float above it for a while, and then dip in and splash again. Finally they rise up (always visible through the layer of the paraffin) and lower themselves sufficiently to place on my hands the still warm paraffin mould. This scene is repeated three times more and after the séance we find three paraffin moulds of clasped hands.

A moment later a marvellous light phenomenon. A light hand moves before the eyes of those present. In its fingers can be seen something like a piece of shining glass. The hand seems to be transparent. We can see the colour of the body. The phenomenon is wonderful, and is repeated three times. Then the hand made of light approaches the face and illuminates it. It is a beautiful male face. I could not observe the details clearly. During this scene the medium, in a trance, held by both hands, did not move at all. The séance finished at 2 am. Dr Geley.

We also have a detailed account by Hewat McKenzie, the Principal of the British College of Psychic Science, who described in detail the experiment which he himself conducted with Kluski at Kluski's apartment in May 1922 (McKenzie 1922-3):

The medium's right hand was held by Mrs McKenzie's left, and the medium's left hand was held by another sitter. The five wax gloves illustrated were produced within about five minutes of the time when the first was laid lightly upon my hand and coat sleeve, and while still in the hot molten state. As it was laid upon my hand several drops of hot wax splashed from it upon my clothes. The remaining four were placed upon the table in close succession, at about one minute interval between each.

The medium, previous to the experiment, was stripped naked and examined by me, in the presence of my interpreter, a gentleman who had never before sat with M. Kluski. The medium then put on another suit of clothes after same had been carefully examined. After the medium and six friends were seated, I was requested to lock the door. A 60-candle power electric lamp illuminated the room for some minutes after the séance began. Soon after this was extinguished, splashing was heard in the molten wax, which was contained in a basin upon the table immediately in front of me, creating a sound similar to what one might expect if a hand or hands were being actively moved amongst the liquid paraffin.

These gloves were without doubt freshly constructed, being soft to the touch when the first one was laid on my arm.

McKenzie also makes the point that the moulds, which can be examined at the College, are in one piece, each of them from a different hand, and all quite unlike the hands of the medium.

The association between the light phenomena and the production of paraffin moulds was observed at a number of séances reported by Okołowicz and summarised here, concentrating on descriptions of the formation of the moulds:

Séance on 23 November 1919:

Participants: Franek Kluski (medium), Ludomira Grzel., Wanda Rydzewska, Stefan Prince Lubomirski, Kazimierz Broniewski, Norbert Okołowicz.

The task was to obtain paraffin moulds, and then to photograph the apparition. At 23:00 all those mentioned took their places at a table in the corner of the study. Melted paraffin in a metal container had been placed in the middle of the table. On the desk, close to the window, was the red electric lamp which stayed on throughout the whole of the séance. The medium and all those present were holding hands. A few minutes after the white light was extinguished, the participants became aware of minor lights and rustles close to the medium. After asking aloud for paraffin moulds of hands, rustles were heard as if of manipulating the hot paraffin. Those facing the red light noticed the shadows of hands appearing as reasonably clear silhouettes above the container of paraffin, in the light of the red lamp.

After a while the number of lights increased; they suddenly began to gather in one place, to the left of the medium, at the height of some 2 metres from the floor, and suddenly formed a large, regular, isosceles triangle made up of lights equidistant from each other and radiating like little stars. The middle of this triangle was filled with a large number of somewhat larger and irregularly scattered lights. This phenomenon lasted a few moments. While observing these lights, familiar rustles indicated that a number of paraffin moulds have been produced and left on the table.

Then, without anybody expressing that wish aloud, the typewriter, standing on the desk in the full light of the electrical red lamp, made a noise. Although the typewriter was close to the light, almost all those present noticed only the very fast movement of the keys, as if pressed by a skilled typist. At the same time the persons sitting next to the medium felt their hands pressed forcefully by the medium, while previously the medium's hands were joined to his neighbours' hands only lightly.

The séance was stopped at 23:30 hrs and, after lighting the white light, three paraffin moulds of hands were found on the table, and in the typewriter a piece of paper with the following sentence: "I am the smile of balance, my poem of love and life has survived epochs".

The summarised excerpts from the séance on 9 January 1924, reported by a participant, a lawyer, Tadeusz Zagórski, report similar phenomena:

Participants: Zygmunt Mostowski, Tadeusz Biliński, Norbert Okołowicz, Karol Sypniewski, Tadeusz Pawłowski and I [the author, TZ].

It began after supper at about 23:00 and lasted about an hour. A hand chain was formed with the participants around the table, on which was a heavy container of paraffin and a well-charged screen. The phenomena started almost immediately. There were touches, movement of objects, and bluish lights flitted and gathered into groups. Soon there was splashing in the paraffin container and a number of participants were splashed, including the writer. Then paraffin moulds were seen on the table. On examination after the séance, these turned out to be perfect forms of human hands, one of which was of two clasped hands. Participants talked among themselves throughout. When someone asked for the paraffin experiment to end and to see phantoms, the screen rose almost immediately and began to circle above the table, showing that the paraffin container was no longer on the table.

The screen rose and showed a phantom of a young Polish officer, recognised as Lieutenant Topór, deceased. The phantom, very clearly visible, seemed to float in the air approaching each participant. This was followed by the form of an Italian officer, also approaching each participant and pointing to the medal on its chest. [...]

Okołowicz comments that this description corresponds generally with his report and the impressions of the other participants. He also describes a very rare phenomenon which took place in the first half of the séance, that of two hands shining with phosphorescent light descending quite visibly vertically from above and immersing themselves in the paraffin container. One of these hands looked like a man's, the other like a child's (the three moulds from this séance were a man's hand, a child's hand, and two clasped female hands).

Okołowicz also published (in *Zagadnienia Metapsychiczne* 1926) a report of new moulds obtained after the publication of his book, at séances on 14 December 1925 and 5 January 1926, excerpts from which are given below:

Before starting the séance some participants mentioned to the medium that it would be good to obtain moulds with the fingers spread wide. After everyone has sat down, the lights are switched off and the chain of hands is formed; the medium very quickly goes into trance (3-4 minutes). The usual noises, knocks, rustles come first. After a short while someone feels the touch of a hand and at the same time little lights appear between the medium and the participant sitting on the medium's left. These lights circle above the table and the container with the melted paraffin which stands in the middle of the table. At one point we see that these lights are the shining fingers of a hand (it seemed to those present that they distinguished the index finger, as well as the second and third fingers). Then the lights stop above the container, disappear, and a moment later we hear the splashing of paraffin. Some participants focus mentally on wanting the mould to be the requested shape, i.e., with the fingers spread out, others express this wish aloud. Paraffin can be heard to splash again and one of the sitters says he was touched on the head with a wet hand. A moment later we hear a light knock on the table and someone else reports that there is a mould before him. The lights keep appearing here and there, we hear the paraffin splash again, and one of the participants is touched by a hand dipped in paraffin. When that participant moves away, saying, "don't splash!" he feels a new mould fall in his lap. The splash is repeated a few more times. The luminous screen, lying on the table, suddenly rises in the air, is turned luminous surface upwards, and the sitters see a hand above its shining surface. The hand is very clear and not transparent. The shapes of the fingers and the palm are very clearly delineated against the screen. This lasts for a few seconds and suddenly we can see the hand become transparent, while at the same time there is a light knock, the mould slides down the screen and falls on the table. The screen turns with its luminous side towards the table, illuminates the mould lying on the table, and is then gently put down alongside it. Wanting to obtain other phenomena, the participants ask the apparitions to take away the paraffin container from the table. A moment later the screen is lifted again, luminous side towards the table, and illuminates the stand on which the paraffin container had been placed. After the séance it was found that the container had been moved onto the floor, above the heads of the participants. Nobody noticed its disappearance from the table. Checking after the sitting, the moulds were in fact found to have the shape of hands with spread-out fingers.

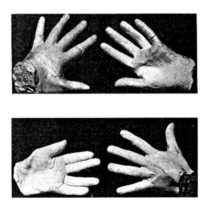

Fig. 5a & 5b: *Casts of paraffin moulds obtained on 14 December 1925 and 5 January 1926.*

At the séance which took place on 5 January 1926 moulds of a similar shape were obtained, although none of those present had a particular wish for such a result and did not ask the medium for it. Comparing the plaster casts obtained from the moulds produced at the two sittings and with similar arrangement of fingers, one can see a significant degree of similarity in the structure of the palm and the fingers and the papillary lines. However, one can also see some differences which allow one to suppose that the "material" used during the séance on 14 December 1925 for creating the mould with fingers spread wide underwent a kind of evolution and, during the sitting on 5 January 1926, to some extent changed the arrangement of the papillary lines while preserving the general character of the hand reproduced on 14 December 1925.

Photographs of the plaster casts [...] convey only a very general idea of the similarities and differences between the moulds. This can only be observed by close visual comparison of the two casts.

In order to highlight the moments during the séance when the process of mould formation takes place, Okołowicz quotes an excerpt from the report describing the second séance, which took place on 5 January 1926.

On the table we placed a container with hot paraffin. A few minutes after the light was extinguished we could hear the splashing of the paraffin. An invisible hand touched the hands of those present, smearing them with paraffin. After a while we heard the sound of a mould falling on the table. Again we heard splashing over quite a long period, and then steps towards one of the lady participants in whose lap the still warm paraffin mould was placed. Afraid of squashing it, the lady asked the invisible apparition to move the mould into a safer place and this was done immediately.

A moment's silence, and then splashing again. The apparition takes up the luminous screen and puts on it a hand with paraffin sticking to it. Then, leaning the screen at an angle on the table, it lightly slides the empty mould along it. We did not see the whole apparition, only the hand and part of the forearm. After a moment's silence invisible hands reach, above the heads of those present, to the table and take away the paraffin container, placing it further in the room.

Participants: Z. Okołowicz, E. Polińska, M. Wnorowska, I. Zaruska, General K. Holy, O. Hubicki, T. Pawłowski, Dr W. Poliński, K. Sypniewski, General M. Zaruski.

Regardless of the effort put into producing them under controlled conditions, and the unlikelihood of any normal explanation for their origin, the paraffin moulds did not become the Permanent Paranormal Object so longed for by Geley. But the very impossibility of explaining their origin – as opposed to explaining them away by ignoring the most salient facts about it – brings us back to the question: what is impossible?

CHAPTER 4

PHYSICAL MEDIUMSHIP: THE PATH TO OTHER REALITIES?

P hysical mediumship of Kluski's magnitude is rare. It is so rare as to seem totally improbable. The witnesses may be impeccable, the reports meticulous, and the safeguards against fraud or illusion perfect, but the phenomena still seem to be a logical impossibility. Yet they are not unique and seem to be the extreme end, and a particular configuration, of a spectrum of essential elements which are part of much more widely reported phenomena. Sherlock Holmes' famous maxim, "when you have eliminated the impossible, whatever remains, *however improbable*, must be the truth" (Conan Doyle, *The Sign of Four*), has usually been applied in order to eliminate the phenomena by assigning all of them to cheating or malobservation. Yet, challenging as it is to the prevailing worldview, the evidence of the séance room viewed in a larger context may lead to discovering important truths about the limits and the nature of consciousness.

Parallels to the anomalous events which centred around Kluski can be found in a variety of circumstances, over cultural and temporal distance, from poltergeist reports, through mediumship, to the after-effects of Near Death Experiences (Rousseau 2011). The striking similarity between the phenomena of mediumship and poltergeist activity has been noted previously (Rae Heath 2011; Colvin 2010), as has the universal appearance of poltergeists through time and through cultures (Gauld & Cornell 1979). In their classic volume *Poltergeists*, Gauld and Cornell analyse and divide into categories a large number (500) of historical and modern cases going back as far as the sixteenth century. The recurring phenomena include most of those observed in physical mediumship: raps and noises, objects moving by themselves (appearing in mid-air or arriving from nowhere), levitations, small animals, human hands, misty figures, luminous effects, malfunctioning electrical equipment, and extrasensory communication among the living and between the living and the phenomena.

Much research has been devoted to various aspects of poltergeist manifestations, including the fact that they often centre around a young person ('agent') entering puberty. However, there are also cases where no particular person seems to be involved and/or a whole group may be involved, while older persons can also be the focus of such events.[1] The important factor seems to be the presence of some personal crisis. What role the human factor plays in generating the phenomena remains a subject of speculation (e.g., hormonal, sexual energy), but something beyond the conventional physical energies as we know them must play a part in events which have physically observable consequences, and therefore must involve such energies, yet the ways in which they behave are very different from our expectations in everyday life. While in poltergeist cases the crisis situation may be temporary, it has been observed by a number of researchers that people with psychic abilities are often reported to have suffered trauma of some kind to their body, such as injury, or electric shock (Carpenter 2004; Jawer 2006) with possible neurobiological effects. As early as 1920 Carrington emphasised the importance of "the pathological condition of the medium", either mental or physical. According to him, this was a feature of nearly all genuine cases. He postulated that "the nervous force which actuates the body might, under certain exceptional circumstances, extend beyond the periphery of the bodily frame, and exert an influence over the external, material world," while "the intelligence involved is produced as a compound of the consciousness of the sitters" (Carrington 1920: 363, 367, 369). In Kluski, we are undoubtedly dealing with someone who has suffered trauma (a bullet lodged in his body), while the sudden illnesses and

---

[1]   In an analysis of 74 poltergeist cases, William G. Roll (Roll 1977: 386) found
     that the age of the 'agents' ranged from 8 to 78.

equally sudden recoveries, closely associated with his emotional state, might fairly be described as a "pathological condition".

However, the human factors which precipitate poltergeist events need not necessarily be pathological, and a combination of factors, including volition, seems to be involved in the production of mediumistic phenomena. Looking at the Kluski phenomena in the context of what we know about poltergeists and what we know about mediumship, a pattern seems to emerge, with the most widespread characteristics present in many reports of minor events, gradually narrowing down to a few individuals as the phenomena become more extraordinary and spectacular.

One of the most common characteristics of poltergeist reports, as well as those from mediumistic sitter groups, is the presence of what is described as "raps," sounds of unknown origin, reported over centuries as well as in the present day, and ranging "from slight rapping sounds, scratchings and 'sawing' sounds to thunderous banging sounds". In some cases, the raps appear to be a form of communication, capable of responding intelligently to the knocks produced by human interlocutors. Quite a lot of research has been done on the available data and, while there is no definitive answer, one possibility might be the presence of "a mechanism of increasing internal stress", followed by audible relief, with the source of the energy unknown (Colvin 2010).

Unfortunately, no recordings of the sounds produced at Kluski séances exist, and the investigators seemed to pay less attention to describing them than to the more spectacular and meaningful lights and apparitions. Yet "knocks" are the initial feature of most (perhaps all) of the sittings, and are a phenomenon which pursued Kluski in everyday life as well. Okołowicz describes them as coming from various items of furniture in Kluski's apartment, and appearing like a conversation taking place somewhere else. Significantly, the knocks seemed to be linked to the medium, since he experienced them as slight pain and shock. It was also the case that when for some reason (such as loss of concentration by the sitters or the medium being disturbed) the formation of a phenomenon during a séance was interrupted, it would usually "degenerate" into loud knocks and kinetic phenomena – as if no longer being "shaped" into the desired results.

When it comes to kinetic phenomena, both poltergeist and physical mediumship accounts most commonly describe levitation and movements of objects, usually small items (such as a light table). Private physical circles composed of individuals with no apparent special

characteristics can produce raps (sometimes continuing beyond the
séance and the séance room), movements and levitations, as well as
other phenomena, such as occasional luminous material (Gauld 1994).
However, it is in the more spectacular manifestations of some poltergeist cases (which may mean that a degree of physical or emotional
trauma needs to be involved) that we find parallels to the intensity of
kinetic phenomena produced in the early phase of Kluski's mediumship. Such a case comes from Poland; as well as being exceptionally
long-lived and violent, it was also exceptionally well observed, investigated, and documented.

It was not labelled as a poltergeist event in Poland at the time that
the story was reported in 1983, when it first began. There is an excellent
and very detailed account of it in a book by two Polish journalists (Ostrzycka & Rymuszko, 1989)[2]. They not only observed closely the young
girl involved, her friends and her family, over a number of years, but
obtained reports from, and interviews with, numerous witnesses, as
well as doctors, psychologists, physicists and assorted scientists who
over a period of some years investigated the phenomena from various
points of view. At no stage was there any evidence for the presence of
paranormal "entities", but many of the phenomena, and some of the
girl's physical states, bear a close resemblance to what happened in
Kluski's early séances.

The focus of the phenomena was Joanna, a girl aged thirteen at the
time when they began. As in many poltergeist cases, the strange events
followed soon after she suffered stress and trauma (the death of her grand-
mother), followed by an illness (flu). Her temperature would fluctuate
inexplicably, rising very high and then dropping to normal or very low
(this pattern persisted over several years). Following her illness, and a
few weeks before the start of kinetic phenomena, she started to "crackle",
producing strange acoustic effects that sounded like the scratching of
claws or clicking. In fact, what sounds like a description of electrical
discharges which would gradually expand away from the girl were frequently reported by witnesses on later occasions as a prelude to the kinetic phenomena; those present would also report their hair standing on
end, and a shivery feeling associated with the air becoming electrified.

The kinetic phenomena were, from the beginning, of such magnitude
and violence that various authorities, including the police, housing

[2] It was also reported in the UK (Bugaj 1996), but that report relied largely
on the book by Ostrzycka & Rymuszko.

officials, and medical personnel (all closely watched by the media) became involved in trying to diagnose and solve the problem. After the family flat was "trashed" on a number of occasions (witnesses included local authority officials and the police), subsidence was thought to be the cause and the girl and her parents were rehoused, only for the phenomena to return in the new location.

Once Joanna was identified as the focus of the phenomena, she became the subject of a research programme, which is why many of the recorded events took place in medical or research establishments where she was undergoing tests. She bent countless spoons (which in this context seemed to be viewed as the Permanent Paranormal Object), as well as thick cables, both informally and under controlled conditions. Like Kluski, she affected magnetic needles, closed circuits and radio waves, as well as electrical equipment, which would malfunction when she was nearby, causing unexpected difficulties in the testing. At various times assorted doctors, nurses, and scientists witnessed such events as an armchair (with Joanna in it) travelling with such force that three adult men could not stop it, equipment being thrown about, and a couch with the girl, two nurses and a doctor sitting on it rising in the air. Objects flew too fast to be observed, along impossible trajectories, defying the force of gravity. One observer described a glass on the table suddenly "undulating", like shimmering hot air, then disappearing with a loud noise and hitting a wall. On an occasion when Joanna was very upset, a washbasin was ripped off the wall, its metal supports torn and buckled, the faucet twisted, with plenty of independent witnesses arriving after they heard the bang. In a hospital, two people witnessed a mirror disappear from the wall in a toilet which was being cleaned, only to immediately shatter in Joanna's room next door, glass from it whirling in the middle of the room.

Unlike Kluski and the participants in his sittings, Joanna was sometimes hurt quite badly by the effects of the phenomena, such as flying glass, and witnesses were on occasion hit by flying objects as well.

Like Kluski, she displayed telepathic abilities, confirmed both formally by tests and by the girl's teacher, who observed that if she formulated the answer to the question asked of the girl in her own (the teacher's) mind, Joanna would answer using sentences very similar to the teacher's style. In a maths class, the girl wrote down on the blackboard the wrong answer but the right one for the equation that the teacher was mentally working on at that time. When interviewed, she said she was not trying to work out the answer, but concentrated on the teacher and the answer popped into her head.

The phenomena were still continuing at the time the authors published their book (1989). Some of the accounts of later events are strongly reminiscent of the strange behaviour of furniture in some of the early Kluski séances, such as the bathtub in Joanna's family flat climbing onto the dryer, or the frightening scene witnessed by Joanna's schoolfriend, where a wall unit leaned forward, hit Joanna on the back of the head, and then straightened itself again, defying the laws of gravity.

We thus have conventional energies behaving very oddly, accompanied by what would be regarded as paranormal phenomena: tremendous kinetic forces without an obvious source, objects travelling along impossible trajectories, levitating and defying gravity, matter moving through matter as in mediumistic apports, electrical disturbances and mental psychic phenomena, all taking place in everyday situations. Apart from occasional references to the paranormal in tabloid titles at the time, the involvement of "otherworldly" entities was not considered as a hypothesis by the investigators, who concentrated on the phenomena and on the girl's physical condition.[3] In fact, all the tests were inconclusive and apart from the strange fluctuations of temperature, both physically and psychologically, she appeared to be an ordinary teenager.

The phenomena produced during the Kluski séances, even when violent, never caused harm to anyone. They also underwent development, much of it in accordance with the sitters' wishes, leading to the conclusion that the medium and the séance participants increasingly learned to control and channel the energies involved, whatever they were. However, in Kluski's case there is at least one other element which does not seem to fit in with what we know of energies or physical bodies and that is the strange phenomenon of lights which on occasion were seen to surround Kluski, to travel underneath his skin, and to leave temporary stains on the surfaces they touched. While the glowing lights and the smell of ozone bring to mind the effects of electrostatic fields (Stevens, 1996), these physically observed emanations seem to be beyond anything normally experienced.[4]

---

[3] Even so, a prominent representative of the scientific establishment admonished the late Dr Roman Bugaj for participating in investigations of this kind, regarding it as a kind of betrayal of science (Dr Bugaj, personal communication).

[4] If the lights and their subsequent materialisations were hallucinations, they would hardly be able to leave paraffin wax gloves behind.

Light phenomena are not unique to Kluski (Alvarado 1987), but there are not many detailed and reliable reports of phenomena of equal intensity and variety. Perhaps those closest to Kluski, both in the quality of manifestations and quality of reporting, are those produced by the Icelandic medium Indridi Indridason (1883-1912) (Gissurarson and Haraldsson 1989, Haraldsson 2011, Haraldsson 2012, Swatos and Gissurarson 1997). His career as a medium was also very short, from 1905 to 1909, and, like Kluski's, was discontinued due to illness. Elaborate controls were undertaken, even with a special room designed for the séances by highly educated investigators who maintained meticulous records, and large numbers of witnesses testified to the genuineness of the phenomena. However, as in the case of Kluski, it is the scope of the phenomena which makes fraud a most unlikely explanation.

Indridason's phenomena began with knocks, peculiar crackling sounds, clicks, and kinetic events involving levitation and pieces of furniture climbing on top of one another, very much in the manner of Kluski's early séances, although there seems to have been much more violence. Another similar feature is the fact that some phenomena also took place outside the séances. However, it is the quantity and quality of lights, often resulting in materialisations, which show the most important parallels:

> [The self-luminous lights] had somewhat different color, some were very white, others were more reddish. Once, during an experimental séance at my home, 58 lights were counted. These lights were of various shapes: some of the lights were round while others were oblong. They were of different sizes: some were small, about an inch in diameter, but others were stripes of light around two to four feet long... (Swatos & Gissurarson 1997: 87).

The lights were closely connected to materialised entities which, again as in the case of Kluski, could be touched, as well as engaging in conversations and embracing the sitters. The most significant phantom was that of a man which:

> ...always appeared as a luminous, beautiful light-pillar, just above the average height of a human figure and slightly broader. Inside this light we saw a human form but it was not clear enough, for example, for the facial expression to be distinctly seen. This light-pillar was very white but with a little tinge of blue. It was very luminous but

did not flicker. However, it did not radiate much light. We saw the medium when the light-pillar stood near where he was sitting in a trance although otherwise there was darkness in the room. (Swatos & Gissurarson 1997: 94)

That particular figure became a frequent visitor and gave its name and details of its life, later identified as accurate, thus providing us with one of the most remarkable cases in the annals of psychical research (Haraldsson 2012).

A number of Indridi's physical characteristics parallelled those of Kluski; thus, Indridi's body emitted strange heat, and when he was ill a fragrance emanated from his head, hands, and arms. As his health deteriorated, his ability to produce lights and full materialisations declined, although parts of a human body were still often seen and felt.

Lights and partial materialisations of hands and heads of different sizes continue to be reported in modern séances (Browning 2013), while an anthropologist researching spiritualist séances finds himself observing "apparent transfigurations of the medium's face and torso" (also observed by others) which leads him to ask "how can an apparently subjective phenomenon be witnessed by more than one individual?" (Hunter 2011: 38). It is easy to find confirmation that the phenomena of physical mediumship have neither disappeared nor significantly changed since their early days. However, a search for evidence of such quality as can stand up to scientific scrutiny regardless of the passage of time and our expanding knowledge takes one back more than a century.

By the time Kluski appeared on the scene in 1919, psychical research had accumulated a wealth of information about, and well-established procedures for, investigating mediumship. It had also attracted a number of highly qualified scientists who saw mediumistic phenomena as a new and exciting branch of knowledge, and who went to great lengths to create conditions for eliminating the possibility of fraud, for observing and recording the phenomena, and for experimenting to establish their range. One such scientist was Filippo Bottazzi, a professor of physiology who, together with a team of equally impressively qualified doctors and physicists, carried out a series of experiments with Eusapia Palladino in 1907 at the Royal University of Naples (Bottazzi 1909/2011). Like many others, he was initially a non-believer, and decided to conduct experiments in his own laboratory with his trusted colleagues and in sufficient lighting to clearly see the medium and the participants. The experiments were aimed at obtaining instrumental recordings of events, instead of relying just on human evidence. In this they were successful, but it is the personal descriptions which are relevant to the Kluski evidence, such as the descriptions of Eusapia's mediumistic hands: "They were pale and diaphanous fingers and hands which might have pearly appearance and brightness. Some appeared above Eusapia's head... at other times they appeared isolated on the arms or shoulders of people close to the *medium*, while they felt touched, pulled by their clothes, hit, or caressed on their head and face." Sometimes the hands would appear to be of normal size, at other times as much as three times as large as Eusapia's hands and arms; they would be skin-coloured, translucent or black; sometimes they seemed to appear just for the sake of being seen, while at other times they would perform physical tasks. They seemed to emanate from Eusapia's body; a witness saw another arm coming out of her shoulder, while Bottazzi describes the occasion when he saw a hand retreat in an arc, "as if entering back into Palladino's body" (Bottazzi 1909/2011: 59; 165-6).

As with Kluski (who seemed able to switch off a light by either producing an elongated extra hand or without any visible intervention), these hands and arms did not seem necessary. Bottazzi describes an experiment where he closely watched and held Eusapia's fingers (which were making appropriate coordinated movements), while another observer watched a mandolin placed at least 50 cm away playing by itself, without any additional limb being formed. Imprints were also produced on clay placed at some distance from Eusapia while Bottazzi held her fingers which were pressing on the table. Levitations, lights, and partial materialisations were regularly observed; while hands, busts gliding between people and vanishing in the middle of the table (sometimes not fully formed and sometimes malformed), appear in accounts of other experiments conducted by other researchers, but with attention to detail similar to that of Bottazzi (Carrington 1909). Ascribing all these phenomena to fraud will simply not do; both Carrington and Ochorowicz (the latter seems to have really liked Eusapia, describing her as a lively "likeable rascal" when he first met her in 1893), investigators with experience of conjuring, found her cheating to be so primitive and obvious as to be incapable of fooling anyone. On the other hand, manifestations such as placing objects in precise required positions in complete darkness (e.g., placing a glass of water to the sitter's lips) and responding to unspoken requests would demand extraordinary abilities of even the most skilled magician, while the presence of permanent traces such as clay impressions or recorded graphs rules out the suggestibility of the sitters as an explanation.

Significantly, Eusapia's physical condition included a scar on her head, caused by a fall when she was one year old. According to Ochorowicz, she sensed pressure and unpleasant irritation in the left side of her head, particularly during storms, when she would also suffer from dizziness. The after-effects of séances included a state of distress, confusion, loss of memory, weakness, digestive troubles, and nausea, as well as a great thirst after a séance.

A number of researchers noted that the mental aspect of Eusapia's phenomena reflected the thoughts, attitudes, and skills of the sitters (as well as her own), once she was attuned to them. For example, Ochorowicz tells us that John King, Eusapia's "control", was able to understand Polish when the sitters were Polish and could suddenly not only write, but write in Russian when the circle was joined by a Russian-speaking writing medium, as well as developing a Cossack connection on the basis of a sitter's memories.

This brings us to the concept of a group mind at work. In the case of Eusapia the mental input reflected in her creations did not have a specific direction. However, we have evidence of just how much can be achieved in this respect by a group of people with no particular views, but united by enthusiasm, mutual rapport, lack of inhibitions and a common goal. In an experiment conducted by a number of members of the Toronto Society for Psychical Research in the 1970s, it was decided to deliberately produce a collective hallucination of a ghost. In order to make sure that it was purely a creation of their own minds, the group invented a character they named 'Philip', with a historical background, hoping to eventually produce a thought-form based on the story they created. There were no psychic claimants among them (which does not mean none of them had psychic abilities), and the sittings took place in the light, with the sitters hoping eventually to see thought forms. The thought forms never materialised (although mistiness was reported on occasion), but raps and scratchings, levitations, movement of objects, and the table dancing and tilting in various ways, became a regular occurrence, as did communicating with Philip. Philip's responses were closely related, and limited to, the knowledge, thoughts, moods, and focus of the sitters, and never went beyond what could be gained from the minds of the sitters (Owen & Sparrow 1976).

It may thus be possible to trace the beginnings of a pattern, starting with ordinary people with no special gifts or characteristics, who are having uninhibited fun and producing, almost as a byproduct, raps, movement of objects, and levitations. Descriptions of the exuberance of inanimate objects, and their responsiveness to the thoughts and emotions of the humans involved, are abundant in accounts of spontaneous "table-turning"[5]. While such events are unusual, in the context of the phenomena discussed here they seem a relatively minor extension of our ability to achieve such results by familiar means. We are now familiar with cutting-edge interface technology which enables paralysed people to manipulate physical objects without the use of muscles and, although this may not be the route to explain such phenomena, it certainly makes the idea of a signal, and an energy, that under some conditions can reach further than expected, somewhat less improbable.

In contrast, cases of involuntary and often destructive interaction between humans and physical objects do not involve much fun, and seem to be associated with personality problems and stresses of various kinds. The case of Joanna, described earlier in this chapter, may be at the extreme end of the spectrum but it is not unique in terms of violence and destructiveness, and she was also capable of controlling her powers sufficiently to produce an endless string of bent metal objects (another often reported anomalous phenomenon). Reports of anomalous relationships between humans and equipment of various sorts, mainly electrical, often by people who have undergone Near Death Experiences, are quite widespread, including the famous physicist Wolfgang von Pauli, who was also famous among his co-workers for the disastrous "Pauli force" which would affect the equipment as soon as he walked into a laboratory (Beauregard & O'Leary 2007: 325). There may be no satisfactory explanation for events of this kind at present, but aspects of electromagnetic sensitivity are part of mainstream research, which may provide the answer to anomalies of this kind.

It is when we come to lights, especially those which turn into walking, talking apparitions, that we step so far outside our ordinary experience as to recoil from this "boggle threshold." Yet we accept the existence of rare diseases on the basis of very few cases, so perhaps this would be the right approach to the few individuals whose spectacular "symptoms" seem to develop in a similar way. Eusapia Palladino may have been the medium who was investigated most thoroughly, but Stainton Moses, the Anglican clergyman whose notes were edited and published by Frederic

---

[5] A 19th-century account tells us about a stool being made to display pride by reaching up, and continuing to do so on its own (Walsh, 1858).

Myers (Myers 1893-4, 1896-7), seems to have been the source of light phenomena strikingly similar to those of Kluski, while "pseudopods" were seen to form near Stella Cranshaw, a non-professional medium thoroughly investigated by Harry Price (Price, 1973: 106-8). The phenomena produced by D.D. Home, perhaps the most famous medium of them all, while never subjected to laboratory research, were extensively investigated by William Crookes (Medhurst et al 1972) who paid much attention to measurable phenomena such as the movement and levitating of objects, as well as being observed by numerous, diligent and sometimes hostile witnesses (Krasiński 1857/1971/1991, Tyutcheva 1859/1975).[6] Home's séances would usually start with cracklings, oscillations, and raps. There would be levitations of persons and objects, and frequent "luminous appearances," sparks, lights responding to questions, nebulous clouds condensing to form hands, seen to do so in good light and becoming hazy at the wrist or the arm, as well as fully formed phantoms (Jenkins 1982:60, 155; Medhurst et al 1972: 118-119, 121, 154-55). As with the Kluski hands, the Home hands could feel and appear different on different occasions, sometimes "icy cold" and sometimes "warm and life-like", seeming to dissolve into vapour at being firmly grasped. Another witness described the effect of their touch "like something between a material touch and a small shock from an electric current" (Tyutcheva 1928-9: 176-7). Other similarities to Kluski include sparks coming from Home's fingers, a phenomenon observed outside séances, as well as his highly emotional personality, traumatic events in childhood, and the frequent illnesses from which Home suffered all his life.

Other examples of well-attested reports could be quoted, but the ones given already might be enough to demonstrate that Kluski's uniqueness lies not in the phenomena themselves; rather, it is the fact that they combine almost the full continuum of all the phenomena of interest to psychical research, both physical and mental, which develop in a progressive and cohesive manner. Uncontrolled kinetic and auditory anomalies common in poltergeist cases proceed towards structured displays of lights and materialised entities, which develop further to represent what seems like embodiments of spiritual beliefs.

---

[6] Much of the "evidence" against D.D. Home came from people who objected to the phenomena on *a priori* grounds. The hostile witnesses referred to here also objected to them most profoundly, but instead of denying their existence they ascribed what they experienced to contact with "lower spirits".

While poltergeist cases sometimes involve raps producing intelligent responses, with Kluski, the mental phenomena of telepathy reach the level of minds acting together on the material world in a way which makes it difficult to distinguish between what is mental and what is physical. All these events are reported in great detail and at first hand by numerous witnesses, some of them experienced investigators.

We are still a long way from answering the question 'what is impossible?' However, the evidence from Kluski's séances provides some clues to where one might begin looking for the interface between the everyday world that most of us know, and whatever might lie beyond. Part of the challenge of Kluski is that one cannot pick and choose the aspect for which to provide a theoretical framework; we need something much, much bigger. Stephen Braude's comment, "No amount of fiddling with random event generators promises the insights that could be gleaned from a medium the calibre of Home or Palladino" (Braude 1986: 65), is perhaps even more applicable here. There is no intention to denigrate the value of micro-research, but the danger of never looking at the big picture is that one might lose sight of it altogether.

And the big picture provided by the Kluski séances includes a strange mixture of aspects of the physical world, the world of imagination, and what seems like other worlds we do not normally encounter. If a group of people acting in rapport can create a communicating entity, as in the case of 'Philip,' without the aid of a powerful medium, then it is less surprising that a group of people acting in unison *with* such a medium can achieve consistent, repeated narratives with the appropriate entities acting out the stories woven on the canvas of their experience. Kluski's "regular" phantoms are impressively structured and active but, like Palladino's 'John King' control, and like 'Philip', they reflect the knowledge and the behaviour which we might expect from the participants and do not go beyond them: male phantoms kiss the ladies' hands in the Polish fashion of the day, a 'doctor' phantom advises someone with a heart problem to carry on smoking, while the Italian patriot Cesare Battisti, who first appears in Italy, continues to display his patriotic enthusiasm in the same manner on his regular visits to the séances in Poland. The most 'advanced' phantoms, such as the Assyrian/Chaldean archpriest, awe the participants with their dignity and their highly symbolic displays of lights, but otherwise seem to correspond quite closely to the stereotypical images one finds in esoteric literature, and reflect the interest in Eastern religions shared by at least some of the sitters. Other apparitions often seem to be moulded and

135

transfigured by the powers of visualisation exercised by individual participants but, when the participants do not focus on the same aim, the séance can fragment and degenerate into confusion, such as the less than successful attempt to produce paraffin moulds for Geley.

The powers of visualisation and the ability to focus play a vital part in much of human activity, from succeeding in sportsmanship to fighting disease. Mental instructions to ourselves produce patterns in our brains that help us rehearse and thus influence our external actions. The experiment of conjuring up 'Philip' goes quite a long way towards demonstrating how effective the focused effort of imagination by a group working in unison can be. But imagination and creativity cannot be sufficient to produce the results observed in the Kluski séances: apparitions which distribute kisses and blows and which, above all, are able to shape and leave behind physical objects such as wax gloves, interact with the world in a very physical way that requires physical energies.

The concepts of psychic force and paranormal energies have been around for centuries; various versions of them, including subtle bodies or "doubles", have appeared in the writings of many distinguished researchers, from Crookes to Honorton (Alvarado 1981-2), while Randall, in his discussion of the phenomena produced by Stella Cranshaw, suggests the possibility of some kind of interpersonal field effect involving sexuality and the balance of the sexes (Randall 2001)[7].

No ectoplasm was ever observed to emanate from Kluski's body, but there is a great deal of material physicality involved in the production of the phenomena. Lights seem to be the prerequisite to the formation of apparitions (sometimes leaving temporary but very physical fatty and odorous stains), but there is also an abundance of heat: Kluski would sweat profusely during the séances, and waves of heat often emanated from him afterwards, accompanied by enormous thirst, hunger, confusion, and exhaustion (as was the case with Palladino). Frequently there was bodily damage to the medium in the form of haemorrhaging and bruising, yet during séances his body could be observed sitting motionless. The participants also experienced exhaustion after a séance, while the young and healthy ones underwent the strange phenomenon of being "rubbed" by the apparitions, again giving the impression of

---

[7] This might well apply in the case of Eusapia Palladino, while at the Kluski séances the powerful personalities included not only "alpha males", but often also women who were equally powerful in terms of personality, creativity, and imagination, among them writers, actors, and social activists.

physical interaction. We are also told about the wear and tear on the fabrics of the participants' clothing during the séances, and it all sounds as if various transformations are taking place, with energy/material for constructing the phenomena being taken from the environment and from the sitters. On a number of occasions the medium himself seems to provide yet another level of strangeness, with bumps and bruises on his body corresponding to encounters involving the apparitions, such as the one on 27 May 1923, when "Two of the participants, curious about the clarity of the figures, decided to test whether these were just a hallucination. At the moment when the phantom of a young, slight woman illuminated itself close by (at a distance of some 2m from the medium), these persons, without breaking the hand chain, suddenly moved their hands forward in order to touch or grab the phantom. Unexpectedly, their hands hit an obstacle, loudly hitting the phantom on the chest; at the same time the medium shivered, moaned loudly, and for a moment clasped convulsively the hands of the controllers. These participants, having established the reality of the phantom, did not try to repeat the experiment. The figure of the woman stayed for a moment in place and lightly wagged its finger in the light of the screen it held, then showing itself very clearly again a number of times, it disappeared. The next day a bruise, as if after a strong blow, was found on the chest of the medium."

Geley's interpretation of the processes involved was to regard Kluski as the source of "primary substance" (Geley 1927: 39), which acts as the base on which the phenomena are produced. Such an interpretation allows for the learning process which can be observed in the quality and structure of the manifestations as they developed over time. It also fits in with the participants' ability to influence them,[8] and it chimes in with one of Kluski's rare comments on the phenomena that "creation is one" and therefore he felt no worse after producing an animal than a human manifestation (McKenzie 1926-27: 17).

If some human beings, under some conditions, are able to project aspects of their bodies so as to be able to shape them to their will, we seem to enter a world very different from our everyday reality, as well as from our ideas about what other worlds might be like should they

---

[8] Sitters interpreted the apparitions in various ways; one of them, Andrzej Niemojewski, commented that when he was talking to an apparition he had the strange feeling that he was talking to an aspect of himself (Niemojewski 1921).

exist. In many ways, it would be so much neater if one could assign phenomena of this kind to a realm that is purely mental, a realm of events clearly taking place in non-physical space (Carr 2008). However, Kluski's séances do not lend themselves to neat categorisation. What is one to make of someone who can reach to turn off the light either by growing a third arm (with a nebulous gap in it) or just by mental effort? Or an "unfinished" hand with a finger hanging off? Or lights that make strange patterns, turn into limbs and produce lasting physical impressions in the form of paraffin gloves? If Okołowicz is right and no such thing as the "fluid" photographed during Count du Bourg de Bozas' carefully designed and controlled experiment (Fig. 4) ever appeared at other Kluski séances, is this an extreme example of experimenter effect? When it comes to phantoms, some seem to be shaped mainly by the sitters' thoughts, emotions, and desires, and often a number of them appears to fill the same "mould," sharing basic features such as eye sockets, changing and looking more lifelike when the participants focus on them, or being larger or smaller than life size. All this does not easily sit alongside accounts of spontaneous apparitions reported from all over the world. Those, on the whole, tend either not to interact with those who encounter them, or to behave like independent entities. This contrasts with the phantoms at Kluski's séances, which often seem like echoes of the sitters' expectations or desires (often unspoken) being created before them. We seem to be in a realm where the physical and the mental are not as we know them, and these may not be the only categories we need. Where can we fit the phantoms not recognised by the sitters until the arrival of the right person, like "Mr Küster", or the phantom of the dancing Jew? Who was behind the messages received through automatic writing, with the attitudes of the medium but the concrete knowledge belonging only to the dead friend? We are told that Kluski was always aware of invisible life constantly going on around him, of never being alone; perhaps he was tuned into realities not available to most of us.

Perhaps it is time to restore physical mediumship to the status of a subject worthy of serious investigation. Its very messiness, the mixture of mental and physical but not as we know them, may carry profound implications for how we view the role of consciousness in the physical world. Mediums like Kluski are undoubtedly rare. It may be that he, along with a small number of others, represents a class of human beings in whom the body and the mind, or the psyche (for want of more precise words) are not integrated into a single system which enables us to function in the world as we know it. Perhaps phenomena such as the ones described direct us towards looking at the mind as "something like a 'material soul', having energetic, spatial, physical, and mental properties" (Rousseau 2011, 2015 forthcoming). There seems to be a crack, a fault line in Kluski's physical and emotional makeup, through which we get a confusing and tantalising glimpse of other ways of being, other realities which seem to be trying to press their way in. We may not be able to get hold of another Kluski, but there might be ways of probing the edges of such realms. Some home circles and groups seem to find such ways; perhaps it is time for serious-minded but uninhibited researchers to take up table-turning and conjuring up thought forms?

THE END

REFERENCES AND BIBLIOGRAPHY

Alvarado, C.S. (1981-82). PK and body movements: A brief historical — and semantic — note. *Journal of the Society for Psychical Research*, 51,116-117.

Alvarado, C.S. (1987). Observations of luminous phenomena around the human body: A review. *Journal of the Society for Psychical Research*, 54, 38-60.

Beauregard M. & O'Leary, D. (2007). *The Spiritual Brain; A Neuroscientist's Case for the Existence of the Soul.* NY: HarperOne.

Bottazzi, F. (1909/2011). *Mediumistic Phenomena.* Princeton, New Jersey: ICRL Press.

Braude, S. E. (1986). *The Limits of Influence: Psychokinesis and the Philosophy of Science.* London: Routledge and Kegan Paul.

Browning, R. (2013). A report of the relationship between psychical phenomena and electronic voice phenomena reported in seances with a physical circle. *Paranormal Review* 68, 12-21.

Bugaj, R. (1993). *Eksterioryzacja – istnienie poza ciałem [Exteriorisation – Existence outside the Body].* Warszawa: Sigma Not.

Bugaj, R. (1994). *Fenomeny paranormalne [Paranormal Phenomena].* Warszawa: Wyd. Adam.

Bugaj, R. (1996). Macro-PK in Poland: An Account of Two Cases. *Journal of the Society for Psychical Research*, 61, 26-33.

Burton, J. (1948). *Heyday of a Wizard. Daniel Home the Medium.* London: George G. Harrap & Co. Ltd.

Carpenter, J. C. (2004). First Sight: Part one, a Model of Psi and the Mind. *Journal of Parapsychology,* 68, 2, 217-254.

Carr, B. (2008) Worlds apart? Can psychical research bridge the gulf between matter and mind? *Proceedings of the Society for Psychical Research,* 59, 1-96.

Carrington, H. (1909). *Eusapia Palladino and Her Phenomena.* New York: B.W. Dodge & Company.

Carrington, H. (1913). *Personal experiences in Spiritualism (including the official account and record of the American Palladino Seances).* London: T.W. Laurie Ltd.

Carrington, H. (1920). *The Physical Phenomena of Spiritualism.* New York: American Universities Publishing Company.

Carrington, H. (1954) *The American Seances with Eusapia Palladino.* NY: Garrett Publications.

Coleman, M. (1994).Wax-moulds of 'spirit' limbs. *Journal of the Society for Psychical Research,* 59, 340-346.

Colvin, B. G. (2010). The acoustic properties of unexplained rapping sounds. *Journal of the Society for Psychical Research,* 73, 2010, 65-93.

Czubryński, A. (1936-1946). *Stany nadnormalne u świętych. Studium parapsychologiczno-religiologiczne [Supernormal states in saints. A parapsychological-religiological study].* Warszawa: Unpublished manuscript notes.

Dawes, E. A. (1979). *The Great Illusionists.* London: David & Charles.

Dingwall, E.J. (n.d.). *Very Peculiar People.* London: Rider & Co.

Gaskill, M. (2001). *Hellish Nell: Last of Britain's Witches.* London: Fourth Estate.

Gauld, A. (1994). Experiences in Physical Circles. *Psi Researcher,* 14, pp. 3-7.

Gauld, A. and Cornell, A.D. (1979). *Poltergeists.* London: Routledge & Kegan Paul.

Gaunt, P.J. (2012). *Spirit Wax Moulds*. Britten Memorial Museum, Booklet 1.

Geley, G. & De Brath, S. (1927). *Clairvoyance and Materialization: A Record of Experiments*. Kessinger Legacy Reprints. London: T. Fisher Unwin Ltd.

Gissurarson, L.R. and Haraldsson, E. (1989).The Icelandic physical medium Indridi Indridason. *Proceedings of the Society for Psychical Research*, 57, 55-148.

Haraldsson, E. (2011). A perfect case? Emil Jensen in the mediumship of Indridi Indridason, the fire in Copenhagen on November 24th 1905 and the discovery of Jensen's identity. *Proceedings of the Society for Psychical Research*, 59, 195-223.

Haraldsson, E. (2012). Further facets of Indridi Indridason's mediumship, including 'transcendental' music, direct speech, xenoglossy and light phenomena. *Journal of the Society for Psychical Research*, 76, 129-149.

Hunter, J. (2011). Talking with the spirits: anthropology and interpreting spirit communication. *Journal of the Society for Psychical Research*, 75.3,129-141.

Jawer, M. (2006). Environmental sensitivity: Inquiry into a possible link with apparitional experience. *Journal of the Society for Psychical Research*, 70.1,25-47.

Jenkins, E. (1982): *The Shadow and the Light; A Defence of Daniel Dunglas Home the Medium*. London: Hamish Hamilton.

Józefowicz S., Legiewicz R. and Dalborowa R. (1973). Wspomnienia [Reminiscences]. *Stolica* 12, 20, 23.Warsaw.

Karwacka, H. (1982). *Kabaret Artystyczno-literacki „Momus"*. Warszawa: PWN.

Keen, M. Ellison A., Fontana, D. (1999). The Scole Report. *Proceedings of the Society for Psychical Research*, 58.

Kledzik, M. (2003). *W cieniu Ogrodu Saskiego – Królewska 16*. Warszawa: Oficyna Wydawniczo-Dziennikarska.

Krasiński, Z., ed. Z. Sudolski. (1971). *Listy do Konstantego Gaszyńskiego [Letters to Konstanty Gaszyński]*. Warszawa: PIW.

Krasiński, Z., ed. Z. Sudolski (1991). *Listy do różnych adresatów, [Letters to various correspondents].* Vol. 2. Warszawa: PIW.

Lebiedziński, P. (1927). *Studium o mediumiczności p. Marii Przybylskiej, medium audytywnego. [Study of mediumship of Mme Maria Przybylska, an auditive medium].* Paper given by the author at the Third International Congress of Psychical Research in Paris on 28 September 1927, published in *Proceedings of the Institut Métapsychique International Sept-Oct 1927,* Paris 1928, 124-133.

McKenzie, B. (1926-1927). Materialized Animal Apparitions. *Psychic Science,* V, 17-22.

McKenzie, H. (1922-23). Quarterly transactions of the British College of Psychic Science, London, 1,185-187.

McMoneagle, J. (2006). *Memoirs of a Psychic Spy.* Charlottesville: Hampton Roads.

Medhurst, R.G. and Goldney, K.M. (1964). William Crookes and the physical phenomena of mediumship. *Proceedings of the Society for Psychical Research, 54,* 25-157.

Medhurst R.G, Goldney, K., Barrington, M.A. (eds) (1972). *Crookes and the Spirit World.* London: Souvenir Press.

Modrzejewski, T. (1910). *Poezje.[Poems]*

Modrzejewski, T. (1913). *Strzępy Życia. Poezje II.[Scraps of Life. Poems II].* Warszawa: Gebethner i Wolff.

Modrzejewski, T. (1936). *Wyrazy, które umarły i które umierają.* Warszawa: F. Hoesick.

Myers, F.W.H. (1893-4, 1896-7). The experiences of Stainton Moses. *Proceedings of the Society for Psychical Research,* vol. 9 and 11.

Niemojewski, A. (1921). *Dawność a Mickiewicz [Antiquity and Mickiewicz].* Warszawa: Gebethner i Wolff.

Ochorowicz, J. (1887/1996) *O sugestii myślowej [On Mental Suggestion].* Preface by Ryszard Stachowski. Warszawa: PWN.

Ochorowicz, J. (1913-1915). *Zjawiska Medyumiczne [Mediumistic Phenomena].* Warszawa: Biblioteka Dzieł Wyborowych. Unpublished translation by Casimir Bernard.

Okołowicz, N. (1926). *Wspomnienia z seansów z medium Frankiem Kluskim. [Reminiscences of Sittings with the Medium Franek Kluski]* Warszawa: Książnica – Atlas.

Okołowicz, N. (1926). Sprawozdania [Reports] Section II. *Zagadnienia Metapsychiczne*, 9-10.

Ostrzycka, A. & Rymuszko, M. (1989). *Nieuchwytna Siła [The Elusive Force].* Warszawa: Oficyna Literatów "Rój".

Owen, I.M. and Sparrow, M. (1976). *Conjuring up Philip: An Adventure in Psychokinesis.* Ontario: Fitzhenry & Whiteside.

Pajewski, J. (1995). *Budowa drugiej Rzeczypospolitej 1918-1926 [Building the Second Republic of Poland 1918-1926].* Kraków: PAU.

Pawłowski, F.W. (1925) The mediumship of Franek Kluski of Warsaw. *Journal of the American Society for Psychical Research*, 19, 481-504.

Polidoro, M. and Garlaschelli, L. (1997). Spirit Moulds: A Practical Experiment. *Journal of the Society for Psychical Research*, 62, 58-62.

Polski Słownik Biograficzny/Polish Biographical Dictionary (1977). Warszawa: PAN.

Price, H. and Dingwall, E. J. (1922). *Revelations of a Spirit Medium.* London: Kegan Paul.

Price, H. (1933). *Leaves from a Psychic's Case-Book.* London: Victor Gollancz

Price, H. (1939). *Fifty Years of Psychical Research.* London: Longmans, Green & Co.

Price, H. and Turner, J. (1973). *Stella C. An Account of Some Original Experiments in Psychical Research.* London: Souvenir Press.

Rae Heath, P. (2011). *Mind-Matter Interaction.* Jefferson NC: McFarland & Co.

Randall, J. (2001).The mediumship of Stella Cranshaw: A statistical investigation. *Journal of the Society for Psychical Research*, 65, 38-46.

Richet, C. R. (1923). *Thirty years of Psychical Research.* NY: Macmillan.

Rogo D.S. (1980). Theories about PK: A critical evaluation. *Journal of the Society for Psychical Research*, 50, 359-378

Roll W.G. (1977). Poltergeists. In: Wolman, B.B. (Ed.) *Handbook of parapsychology*, N.C.: McFarland & Co., 382-413.

Rousseau, D. (2011). *Minds, Souls and Nature. A Systems-Philosophical Analysis of the Mind-Body Relationship in the Light of Near-Death Experiences.* Unpublished Ph.D. Thesis, University of Wales.

Rousseau, D. (2015 in press). Dualism and Psi. In: May, E.C. & Marwaha, S.B. (Eds). *Extrasensory Perception: Support, Skepticism, and Science. Vol. II (Theories and the Future of the Field).* Westport CT: Praeger Publications.

Rzewuski, S. (1928). Wynik zbiorowych doświadczeń telepatycznych między Atenami a Warszawą. [Results of group telepathic experiments between Athens and Warsaw]. *Zagadnienia Metapsychiczne* 19-20, 36-51.

Sokołowski, T. (1936). Animizm czy spirytyzm? [Animism or spiritism?] *Lotos* 101-103.

Sommer, A. (2012). Psychical Research and the Origins of American Psychology: Hugo Münsterberg, William James and Eusapia Palladino. *History of the Human Sciences*, 25(2) 23-44.

Steinmeyer, J. (2003). *Hiding the Elephant.* London: Arrow Books.

Stevens, P. (1996). *Reconsidering the relationship between electromagnetism and psi.* Society for Psychical Research Conference Abstract.

Swatos, W.H. Jr and Gissurarson, L.R. (1997). *Icelandic Spiritualism: Mediumship and Modernity in Iceland.* New Brunswick USA: Transaction Publishers.

Szmurło, P. (1929). O próbach telepatii między Atenami i Warszawą. [On experiments in telepathy between Athens and Warsaw]. *Zagadnienia metapsychiczne* 23-24, 21-35.

Tyutcheva, A. F. (1853-1882/1975). *Pri Dvore Dvukh Imperatorov, Vospominaniya, Dnevnik, 1853-1882 [At the Court of Two Emperors, Reminiscences, Diary 1853-1882].* Moscow: 1928-9, republished Cambridge: Oriental Research Partners.

Urbański. T. (1984). Zapiski do autobiografii naukowej [Notes for a scientific autobiography]. *Kwartalnik Historii Nauki i Technologii PAN*, XXIX, 1, 7-8.

Varvoglis, M. (2002). The Kluski hand moulds. *Proceedings of the 45th Annual Convention of the Parapsychological Association*, 370-380.

Walsh, Le cte T. (1858). *Dunglas Home et le spiritualisme américaine*. Paris.

Weaver, Z. (1992). The enigma of Franek Kluski. *Journal of the Society for Psychical Research* 58, 289-301.

Wittlin, T. (1996). *Szabla i koń. Gawęda o Wieniawie [The Sword and the Horse. The Story of Wieniawa]*. Łomianki: LTW.

Żeleński T. (Boy) (1958). *Godzina w krainie czarów.[An Hour in the Land of Magic] Felietony*. Warszawa: PIW.

http://archived.parapsych.org/members/e_c_may.html

http://karpaccy.pl/pulkownik-norbert-okolowicz

INDEX

self-illuminating, 59, 60, 81, 82,
86, 87, 102
of animals, 51, 52
the primitive man, 52, 53, 72

O

outside the séance, 21-24, 103, 104
- automatic writing, 27, 32, 62,
63, 64, 65, 66, 67
- change of weight, 47
- clairvoyance, 12, 22, 61, 62
- electrical phenomena 21, 69,
90
- experiments with:
compass; 20, 67
galvanometer, 68
paraffin wax; 78, 98, 99,
108, 109, 110, 111, 115,
116, 117, 118, 119, 120,
121
thoughtography 69
- kinetic; levitations,
movement of objects
20, 30, 45, 46, 70, 71,
90, 91
- lights, kinds of: 20, 34, 35,
47, 48, 49, 50, 89, 128,
129, 130
- odours 21, 51, 90
- out-of-body experiences
12
- telepathy, 60, 127, 135
- sounds, 19, 20, 30, 45, 90,
125, 129
'Philip' experiment:,
- thought forms, 132, 135,
139, 158, 167

P

Piłsudski, Józef, 1, 3, 4, 61, 82
Polidoro, Massimo, 107
Polish Society for Psychical
Research, Polish SPR, ix, xvii,
xviii, 5, 6, 25, 26, 32, 47, 77
Poltergeist, 123-126, 134, 135
Price, Harry, 18, 134
Przybylska, Maria, 6

R

Richet, Charles, 18, 25, 33, 34, 39, 77,
108, 109
Rousseau, David, xiii, 123, 139
Rymuszko, Marek, 126
Rzewuski, Stefan, 5

S

Scole report, xvi
Schiller, Leon, 3, 15
séances:
- conditions; 33, 34, 36, 88
- controls; 33, 38, 39
- lighting 33, 37, 38,
- participants, influence of, 42,
43, 44, 112, 113, 114
- temperature, 38
Sidgwick, Henry, xix
Sidgwick, Eleanor, xix
Sokołowski, Tadeusz, 15, 21, 23, 26,
62, 107
Sommer, Andreas, xx
Society for Psychical Research, SPR,
ix, x, xi, xvii,
Stargate project, 2
Steinmeyer, Jim, xvi
Stpiczyński, Wojciech, 82
Szmurło, Prosper, 5, 6, 87-89, 91,
95
Szyfman, Arnold, 3, 15

Paperbacks also available from
White Crow Books

Jesus of Nazareth with Simon Parke—
Conversations with Jesus of Nazareth
ISBN 978-1-907661-41-9

Thomas à Kempis with Simon
Parke—*The Imitation of Christ*
ISBN 978-1-907661-58-7

Julian of Norwich with Simon
Parke—*Revelations of Divine Love*
ISBN 978-1-907661-88-4

Allan Kardec—*The Spirits Book*
ISBN 978-1-907355-98-1

Allan Kardec—*The Book on Mediums*
ISBN 978-1-907661-75-4

Emanuel Swedenborg—*Heaven and Hell*
ISBN 978-1-907661-55-6

P.D. Ouspensky—*Tertium Organum:
The Third Canon of Thought*
ISBN 978-1-907661-47-1

Dwight Goddard—*A Buddhist Bible*
ISBN 978-1-907661-44-0

Michael Tymn—*The Afterlife Revealed*
ISBN 978-1-970661-90-7

Michael Tymn—*Transcending the
Titanic: Beyond Death's Door*
ISBN 978-1-908733-02-3

Guy L. Playfair—*If This Be Magic*
ISBN 978-1-907661-84-6

Guy L. Playfair—*The Flying Cow*
ISBN 978-1-907661-94-5

Guy L. Playfair —*This House is Haunted*
ISBN 978-1-907661-78-5

Carl Wickland, M.D.—
Thirty Years Among the Dead
ISBN 978-1-907661-72-3

John E. Mack—*Passport to the Cosmos*
ISBN 978-1-907661-81-5

Peter & Elizabeth Fenwick—
The Truth in the Light
ISBN 978-1-908733-08-5

Erlendur Haraldsson—
Modern Miracles
ISBN 978-1-908733-25-2

Erlendur Haraldsson—
At the Hour of Death
ISBN 978-1-908733-27-6

Erlendur Haraldsson—
The Departed Among the Living
ISBN 978-1-908733-29-0

Brian Inglis—*Science and Parascience*
ISBN 978-1-908733-18-4

Brian Inglis—*Natural and Supernatural:
A History of the Paranormal*
ISBN 978-1-908733-20-7

Ernest Holmes—*The Science of Mind*
ISBN 978-1-908733-10-8

Victor & Wendy Zammit —*A Lawyer
Presents the Evidence For the Afterlife*
ISBN 978-1-908733-22-1

Casper S. Yost—*Patience
Worth: A Psychic Mystery*
ISBN 978-1-908733-06-1

William Usborne Moore—
Glimpses of the Next State
ISBN 978-1-907661-01-3

William Usborne Moore—
The Voices
ISBN 978-1-908733-04-7

John W. White—
The Highest State of Consciousness
ISBN 978-1-908733-31-3

Stafford Betty—
The Imprisoned Splendor
ISBN 978-1-907661-98-3

Paul Pearsall, Ph.D. —
Super Joy
ISBN 978-1-908733-16-0

**All titles available as eBooks, and selected titles available in Hardback and
Audiobook formats from www.whitecrowbooks.com**

Lightning Source UK Ltd.
Milton Keynes UK
UKOW04f1923270315

248679UK00004B/140/P